USING

WITH R:BASE 3.1 / 3.0™

USING

WITH R:BASE 3.1 / 3.0™

JANET R. WILSON
Seattle University

PATRICIA A. SHEPARD
Bellevue Community College

WCB Wm. C. Brown Publishers

Book Team
Editor *Kathy Shields*
Software Hotline and Developmental Support Technician *Lisa Schonhoff*
Production Coordinator *Peggy Selle*

Wm. C. Brown Publishers
President *G. Franklin Lewis*
Vice President, Publisher *George Wm. Bergquist*
Vice President, Publisher *Thomas E. Doran*
Vice President, Operations and Production *Beverly Kolz*
National Sales Manager *Virginia S. Moffat*
Advertising and Marketing Manager *Ann M. Knepper*
Editor in Chief *Edward G. Jaffe*
Managing Editor Production *Colleen A. Yonda*
Production Editorial Manager *Julie A. Kennedy*
Production Editorial Manager *Ann Fuerste*
Publishing Services Manager *Karen J. Slaght*
Manager of Visuals and Design *Faye M. Shilling*

Cover design by Sailer & Cook Creative Services

Library of Congress Catalog Card Number: 90-84172

ISBN: 0-697-12821-0

Printed in the United States of America by Wm. C. Brown Publishers,
2460 Kerper Boulevard, Dubuque, IA 52001

10 9 8 7 6 5 4 3 2 1

TABLE OF CONTENTS
SQL for R:BASE 3.0

PREFACE

AUDIENCE

This text is intended to be used at the college level by students who have familiarity with computers and who have completed at least the intermediate level of R:BASE. It is intended to be used as an introduction to the use of SQL (Structured Query Language) commands using R:BASE. The text is designed to enable a student to work through the lessons on his/her own, or it may be used in a more traditional classroom setting. The text was written to be used in software application classes at the four-year or community college level, or in adult education classes. It might also be effective at the high school level in some advanced classes; this, however, is not the intended audience and so is up to the individual instructor.

APPROACH

A step-by-step approach guides students through the various procedures used to produce, modify, view, and query realistic database tables using SQL. This means that students will be "learning by doing," which includes making some mistakes. The text anticipates these "errors" and includes responses and solutions to possible problems that may arise during students' work with SQL.

Upon completion of this text, the student will be familiar with nearly all of the commands in SQL with R:BASE. The text reinforces that learning by repeating commands as well as by introducing new features in each subsequent part. Learning is also reinforced with recall questions and practice documents included at the end of most parts.

FEATURES

Each part includes chapters covering related procedures.

Part 1

Chapter 1 SQL With R:BASE
Chapter 2 Relational Database Systems
Chapter 3 A Quick Look at SQL

Part 1 gives students an overview of SQL and its commands as used with R:BASE. It discusses relational database design and shows a sample database. It also gives instructions for using the text.

Part 2

Chapter 4 Beginning to Use SQL Commands
Chapter 5 Creating Indexes

Part 2 gets the students started by using SQL commands to create tables. The students begin immediately to identify primary keys, add columns, enter data values, include NULL values, delete rows, drop tables, and change row values. In addition, students learn the function of indexes and their use in expediting queries. Reinforcement exercises at the end of this part give the students additional practice in creating their own tables, creating indexes, and assigning primary key columns.

Part 3

Chapter 6 Performing Single-Table Queries
Chapter 7 Performing Multi-Table Queries

Part 3 uses the tables created in Part 2 to begin queries, the most useful aspect of SQL and relational database design. Students begin by performing single-table queries using the SELECT command for retrieving specific or all columns of a table and for retrieving columns in a specific order. They also apply the DISTINCT argument, the WHERE clause, the BETWEEN, LIKE, and IN operators, the GROUP BY and ORDER BY clauses, and the HAVING clause. Reinforcement exercises are included at the end of Chapter 6. Chapter 7 walks the students through multi-table queries. In this chapter, they learn to join two tables and more than two tables. Students learn to perform subqueries and to apply the IN and EXISTS operators. They also practice using the ANY or SOME commands and the ALL command. Reinforcement exercises again allow the students to practice skills by performing multi-table queries on other tables they have created.

Part 4

Chapter 8 Creating Views

Part 4 introduces the student to the concept and creation of views. They learn to create views of specific columns, update views, query views, group views with COUNT and SUM, join two or more tables in views, and drop views. They also practice updating views. Reinforcement exercises give students additional practice with views.

Part 5

Chapter 9 Determining User Privileges
Chapter 10 Global Features of SQL

In this part, students are introduced to the commands used in a global R:BASE environment, such as network and mainframe environments. Commands discussed include the use of GRANT and REVOKE privileges and creating new names for tables.

Part 6

Chapter 11 Using SQL in Programs

This final part discusses the use of embedded SQL commands. It gives a broad overview of commands used in general terms, including how to insert data values into program variables, declaring variables, and retrieving data values into variables. It also discusses the use of SQL commands as embedded into a COBOL program.

Preview Each chapter begins with a preview of the commands to be learned that includes a description of the commands, possible uses of the commands, and other general comments pertinent to each particular application.

Step-by-step instructions Following the preview are exercises leading the student through the steps necessary to create, modify, change and otherwise work with a table using the specific commands in that chapter. In the step-by-step directions, SQL commands are shown indented and appear typed horizontally across the width of the screen as they would appear to the students typing them. Headings are printed in 12 point, bold, all caps, and indicate a specific feature to be covered. Subheadings are printed in 12 point, bold, first letter capitalized, and indicate step-by-step instructions for using that feature. *"Notes"* are additional comments, information, or explanations of possible problem areas and are shown in italics.

Reinforcement exercises Reinforcement exercises are included at the end of most parts. These exercises consist of recall questions intended to assist the student in understanding the commands learned in the preceding exercises. By answering the questions, the student is able to summarize and recall the steps used for each feature. Following the recall questions are practice exercises that enable students to apply the commands learned to actual table production, further reinforcing their learning.

Quick reference guide Appendix I is a quick reference guide. This guide summarizes the sequence of commands used for the various functions and lists them in alphabetical order. Students are encouraged to use this guide as a prompt, rather than returning to the specific exercises for assistance in working with their own tables or in working through the practice exercises. The guide was included in this text so that students could refer to it quickly as a reminder of commands learned previously.

Glossary of Terms Appendix II provides the student with a glossary of terms common primarily to SQL but some that are also used in R:BASE. This is intended to give the student reference to some words and commands that may be new or that need further definition.

SQL Command Reference Appendix III consists of a a command reference that includes SQL syntax and syntax diagrams. This is intended to be used for reference by the student to the correct sequence of commands used in the SQL structure.

INSTRUCTOR'S MANUAL

An instructor's manual is included in the package along with the textbook and consists of the following:

* A description of the organization of the text.

* A description of the organization of the instructor's manual.

* An outline of each part, consisting of:
    - Learning objectives
    - Teaching techniques
    - Chapter outlines
    - Lecture outline for each chapter
    - The solutions to the recall questions
    - The solutions to the practice exercises

* A test bank, which includes:
    - A test for each part, 2 through 5
    - A comprehensive test covering parts 2 and 3
    - A comprehensive test covering parts 4 and 5
    - A final test covering parts 2 through 5

* Solutions to the test bank

* A set of transparency masters that display various SQL commands and results of table manipulation.

ACKNOWLEDGMENTS

We wish to thank the many reviewers who provided helpful comments and suggestions, many of which have been incorporated in this text. We also wish to thank Kathy Shields, Peggy Selle, and the excellent staff at Wm. C. Brown Publishers for their guidance and support. They were consistently friendly and encouraging throughout the completion of this project. Family and closest friends are to be thanked for their endurance, patience, and understanding.

Janet Wilson, Seattle University

Patricia Shepard, Bellevue Community College

PART 1
INTRODUCTION

CHAPTER 1
SQL WITH R:BASE

PREVIEW

Structured Query Language (SQL-pronounced "sequel") is a standard language that enables the user to create or query tables in a relational database.

Because of the increasing integration and interrelation of computer systems, the knowledge of SQL to query a database is becoming essential. Since most of the primary database programs use SQL commands, a knowledge of those commands will enable you to create or manipulate database information regardless of the environment - be it personal computer, work station, or mainframe.

In this book, you will use the SQL commands as they are used with R:BASE for 3.0. If you have any familiarity with SQL, you will recognize the similarity with which the commands are entered from the keyboard. If you have no background with SQL, you will find the commands similar to those you enter when giving instructions in R:BASE from the R> prompt. Many of the R:BASE commands are in fact SQL commands. The structure may be slightly different and many new commands will be applied that you would not have used with R:BASE; however, you will still see many familiar words and should easily recognize the layout of the instructions.

SQL COMMANDS

SQL commands are divided into several groups. These groups are not introduced in order in this text; rather, the commands are introduced as they would logically be used beginning with creating a table and adding data to it and moving through modifications and in-depth queries of multiple tables. It is worth noting, however, the differences between the various types of commands used in building the SQL language.

Database Definition Commands:

Database definition commands are used to define the basic structures of a database. They include defining columns, table, and views. The commands included in this category are

ALTER TABLE
COMMENT ON
CREATE INDEX
CREATE SCHEMA AUTHORIZATION
CREATE TABLE
CREATE VIEW
DROP INDEX
DROP TABLE
DROP VIEW

Most of these commands are discussed in this text with the exception of the commands for authorizing use of databases and tables. It is assumed that most of you using this text will be using it with a microcomputer or that the authorization schema will be created and installed by the institution to which you are attached.

Data Manipulation Commands:

Data manipulation commands are used to add, view, and modify data. They are:

DELETE
INSERT
SELECT
UPDATE

Variations of each of these will be used throughout this text.

Data Security Commands:

These commands are used to assign and remove passwords on columns, tables, and views. These commands are not covered in this text because it is assumed that this will be handled uniquely for each instructional environment.

CONNECT
DISCONNECT
GRANT
REVOKE

USING THE TEXT

Instructions in this text are given in the following ways:

1. An overview of the topic to be discussed is given in a brief preview at the beginning of each chapter.

2. Descriptions of a function are given after each subheading introducing the function.

3. Actual steps you are to perform are shown in an itemized list of instructions (1., 2., 3., ...). Many times the instruction will simply begin with the word **Type**, because many SQL instructions are performed in a single set of commands.

4. SQL instructions are shown with command words in uppercase and table names or column names, etc., shown in lowercase. When actually entering SQL commands, you may use all lowercase or all uppercase words. The uppercase wording in this text is used for clarity and quick recognition of SQL command words.

5. When SQL syntax examples are given, the words *table name* or *column name* are shown where you should insert the table or column names.

6 Instructions that need special attention are discussed in *italicized* notes.

To get the most from this text, you should read all information given at the beginning of the chapter and pertaining to each function of SQL discussed. You should also proceed through the text in the order in which the material is presented and cover each topic until it is understood. The information presented will build on itself so that earlier lessons will contain necessary steps for later lessons in the text.

The appendix may be used for reference and include a quick reference guide of SQL examples used in the text, a summary of SQL syntax, and a vocabulary appendix.

CHAPTER 2
RELATIONAL DATABASE SYSTEMS

PREVIEW

To use SQL commands effectively, you must understand the concept of relational database design systems. This section discusses briefly the meaning of a relational database system and gives an example of a simple relational database. This example is used in the early chapters of this text using SQL commands to create the tables.

WHAT IS A RELATIONAL DATABASE?

A database is a system used to store data. If you need only a list of customers' names, addresses, and phone numbers, this information may be kept in one table, and you will not have a relational database. However, if you want to keep a record of the items each customer purchased, the salesperson who made the transaction, a list of all employees, their addresses, and their hiredates, a list of all products carried and their cost to you, then you will need separate tables (or files) for each type of information. These tables should be designed in such a way that information in one table can be used to link that table to another to obtain information that enhances the day-to-day business activities of the organization by querying and joining tables.

It should be remembered, however, that one of the primary advantages of a relational database system is that a minimum of data needs to be repeated from one table to the next. When joining tables so that they may be queried for information, a common column such as customer ID or invoice number may be included from one table to the next. In a small business, these numbers could link tables from inventory through sales. Aside of these common and unique columns, however, other columns such as a description of an inventory item or the customer's name need appear in only one table. To abbreviate, keep a unique identifying column from table to table, but keep only information pertinent to each table after that and try not to duplicate too much information from table to table.

Minimizing redundancy

The primary reason for eliminating the repetition of columns from table to table is that doing so reduces the chances for making errors. For example, if customer name appears not only in the customer table but also in the sales table and in accounts receivable, the chances of making an error in the customer's name somewhere along the line greatly increases. By including the customer name in only one table, the inventory information in another, sales in another, an entry need be made only once at the time of the transaction.

A SAMPLE DATABASE

The following tables have been designed to show a relatively simple relational database. The company, Contemporary Office Interiors, needs information about their customers, about their salespeople, and records of sales. Later on in this text, you will create these tables and add information about product inventories and details of sales transactions. For now, just study the tables and notice the relationship between each. Each table consists of a table name plus several columns. When data is added to the table, each row of data will contain specific information entered in each column, and that information will be different from any other row of data in the table.

custid	name	address	city	state
11	Frances Gates	300 Brighton St.	Seattle	WA
12	Lloyd Ohlsen	103 First Avenue	Seattle	WA
13	Yvonne Lewis	1515 N. E. 50th	Kirkland	WA
14	Dale Glenn	2518 25th N.E.	Redmond	WA
15	Robert Hill	15 Union Rd.	Spokane	WA
16	Rachel Cole	1600 Creekside Dr.	Portland	OR
17	Susan Leland	5157 Caribou Ave.	Anchorage	AK
18	Donn Hansen	900 Deep Freeze Ct.	Fairbanks	AK
19	Jean Randolph	101 Mariposa	Fresno	CA
20	Tom Cranston	15 Seneca St.	Oakland	CA

Table 1 customers

repid	repfname	hiredate	commiss
1	Alex Baldwin	11/5/87	.14
2	Judy Marshall	5/4/89	.12
3	Karen Anderson	7/16/88	.13
4	Roger Maltby	3/10/86	.15
5	Morris Crenshaw	10/21/89	.11

Table 2 salesreps

invid	invdate	repid	custid	netamt	tax	totamt
111	1/7/90	2	15	$350.00	$28.00	
112	1/28/90	1	17	$225.00	$18.00	
113	2/15/90	3	12	$90.00	$7.29	
114	2/23/90	1	16	$150.00	$12.15	
115	2/26/90	4	18	$75.00	$6.08	
116	3/1/90	3	19	$175.00	$14.00	

Table 3 sales

As you can see, the **sales** table contains columns-**repid** and **custid** that are also in the **customers** and in the **salesreps** tables. These columns will be used to link information from one table to information in another table. For example, if you wanted to display the total sales for a particular sales rep, you could enter a SQL query, asking to display all rows in the table **sales** where the **repid** equals a specific identification number for a sales rep. Then, if you wanted to know the names of the customers to whom that particular sales rep had sold products, you could use a SQL query asking to display the names from the **customer** table where the **custid** equaled the identification numbers displayed in the sales rep query. The advantage of using these linking columns such as **repid** and **custid** is that you do not need to duplicate information in several tables. You can enter the customer's name, address, etc., once, then use the **custid** number to access the data after that.

This is an example of the value of a relational database system and gives you an idea of how the database is designed to relate one table to another.

It is not necessary to have rows of information in any particular order. Because you have entered data and identified it with a unique name (or number), the placement of rows of data in a table can be arranged in any way you may want it. By entering the data in no particular order, you can then use a SQL command to display the rows in alphabetical (ascending) order by city or by state, for example. Or you can use a SQL command to display all sales over a certain amount in descending order.

CHAPTER 3
A QUICK LOOK AT SQL

PREVIEW

SQL commands are standard language for accessing and displaying data in relational databases. Because it is a standard language, it can be used in many different database programs. In this text, you will be using R:BASE 3.0.

American National Standards Institute (ANSI) has defined the minimum standards for SQL, and these standards are accepted by the International Standards Organization (ISO) as well. However, SQL does contain some commands that are not recognized by ANSI. For example the command DATE is not an ANSI SQL command, yet because most database programs use DATE to define a column type, SQL has included it as one of its commands.

WHAT ARE SQL COMMANDS?

SQL commands are a collection of instructions that you give at your computer. As mentioned earlier, SQL commands are used within a relational database environment primarily to perform queries on data contained in tables. That environment may be mainframe, minicomputer, or microcomputer, and it may be within the framework of any number of relational database programs. In this book, you will be referencing R:BASE, but SQL could also be used when accessing database programs on a mainframe, or when using any number of programs on a microcomputer. SQL commands were designed to give you flexibility in communicating with any number of relational databases once you have used the commands with one system. In other words, if you become familiar with the SQL commands discussed in this text, you will be able to apply them in other relational database environments as well, with minimum change to the basic structure.

EMBEDDED AND INTERACTIVE SQL

In this text, most of what you will be studying will be *interactive* SQL commands. You may be familiar with performing queries with R:BASE. At the R> prompt, you can give commands that, when invoked, will display information on the screen for you. The SQL interactive commands work the same way. When given, the information is immediately available to the user. Interactive SQL commands are also fairly easy to use and may be learned quickly by those familiar with a relational database program.

Embedded SQL commands are written as part of a high-level programming language such as PASCAL or COBOL. Frequently control is passed from the embedded program commands back to the interactive SQL, and so the combination of embedded and interactive commands may be found.

In this text, the authors assume that most users want to use SQL commands within the structures of their database programs; consequently this text is written from that perspective. Chapter 9 will, however, discuss some of the applications of SQL commands embedded within high-level programs.

SQL CONVENTIONS

You should be familiar with the following conventions and terminology that have special meanings within the framework of SQL.

Arguments:

Arguments complete the meaning of a clause. If a clause begins with the word WHERE for example, then in the clause "WHERE city = 'Seattle' ", "city = 'Seattle' " is the argument.

Clauses:

Commands or statements consist of one or more parts called clauses. Often clauses are looking for conditions or looking for characteristics from the database. A clause may be "WHERE city = 'Seattle' " or "FROM salesreps."

Commands or Statements:

The SQL instructions are given by you to your database program. In this text, the SQL instructions are shown in all capital letters, such as SELECT, CREATE, etc.

Keywords:

Keywords are any words that give instructions in SQL. For example, in the examples above, WHERE and FROM are keywords. A complete list of keywords is included in Appendix II.

Objects:

Objects include any structures in a database program that are given names and stored in memory. Tables, views, and indexes are examples of objects.

NOTES

PART 2
GETTING STARTED

CHAPTER 4
BEGINNING TO USE SQL COMMANDS

PREVIEW

In this chapter, you will start using some basic SQL commands. You will start by creating a table using SQL commands, instead of creating a table from your database program. This chapter also discusses altering tables and dropping tables. These SQL procedures will give you the basics for creating additional tables if you wish or for changing the table structure or deleting a table. Chapter 5 will cover querying the tables you have created. Throughout this text, you will be using SQL commands consistently. Later, if you want to practice querying other tables, that were created using your database program, you may use the same procedures.

All SQL commands are given at the R> prompt. We will assume after this chapter that you know that all commands are given in this way and so it will be mentioned only once.

A *primary key* is a column in a table that uniquely identifies each row. Generally speaking, each row in a table has no particular order. It doesn't need to have an order because you are going to expect the table to have a great deal of flexibility when performing queries. Because of this lack of order, however, you need to have a *primary key* that uniquely identifies each row. Usually, the *primary key* column contains a number, such as *student id* or *customer id.* Numbers are often unique to a table and therefore are good to use. Social security numbers are a good example of unique numbers and that could be a primary key field. By using a unique value, the database system guarantees that no two rows are going to be exactly alike and possibly cause redundancy of data. Also, when a specific row of data is needed, it can be referred to by the primary key. It is a good idea, then, to identify the primary key when you create a table.

The *primary key* in SQL is identified by using the BUILD KEY or CREATE INDEX command. In your first exercise, the key will be identified through the BUILD KEY command simply to emphasize the use of the term *primary key.* After the three tables used in this text are created, you will also learn about building an index.

CREATING TABLES

New tables are created using the CREATE TABLE command. This command creates an empty table, much as would happen if you were using R:BASE. With this command, you also define a set of columns and data types as well as the size of the columns. The data types you may use correspond to those used when creating a table from your R:BASE program. The types used with R:BASE are the standard ANSI types and are listed in Appendix III.

As with R:BASE, the names of tables must be different. In this initial exercise, you create the three tables given as samples of relational database shown below and in Chapter 2. Although tables must have different names; columns within tables may have the same name, and as mentioned in Chapter 2, this may be desirable if you wish to "link" tables through like columns, such as a column called "custid."

To Create a Table

As you would when using the R:BASE main menu, you must define the database before creating tables. Tables will then be entered into the database. From the R:BASE main menu,

1. Create a database called MASTER.

2. Return to the R> prompt with the database, MASTER, open.

You are now ready to create the table and columns and to define the data types. The customer identification will be used as an integer, and all other columns will be text columns in your first table, called **customers.** (*Note: You may use either TEXT or CHAR in a SQL command. Because you would normally use TEXT in R:BASE and are familiar with it, it will be used in the instructions to identify a character or text column.*) An integer column contains number values that will not need a decimal notation and may not be used in calculations as stated in Appendix III. Character columns should always show the maximum width you will need. Numeric columns, however, are assigned a width automatically by the system if no width is specified. This method is easiest since the width of numerical values often changes.

Enter the column names and type using the following procedure:

* Enter one column name, the width, and restrictions for the column. Separate the columns with commas. While this is not necessary, it makes for easier reading and proofing.
* Type all SQL commands in CAPS and all column titles and definitions in lowercase. Again, this is not necessary, but it greatly improves the readability and thus the editing time when entering strings of commands.
* Type the instruction all the way to the right margin and let it automatically wrap to the next line. Do not worry if your line wraps differently from those shown in the examples. Remember, do not press the Enter or Return key until the very end of the instruction.
* Proof the instruction carefully before pressing Enter. Once you press Enter, you must retype the entire instruction again if any errors appear. If errors do appear, use your cursor to move to the position of

the error and correct it by typing over it, pressing the insert (INS) key on the keyboard and inserting characters, or using the delete or Del key to remove unwanted characters, just as you would in any other mode.

3. Type:

```
CREATE TABLE customers custid INTEGER NOT NULL,
    fname TEXT(20) NOT NULL, address TEXT(25), city
    TEXT(15), state TEXT(2)
```

Note: You have the option of either spacing after each comma or not spacing. Do whichever will make it easier for you to type and proof. If you are using an earlier version of R:BASE, you may also have the option of entering the width without parentheses (example: TEXT 20).

4. Press: **Enter**

The NOT NULL constraint prevents a row from ever having a NULL value (or no data entry) in the column. This is a security measure in columns where you must have data values. The **custid** column is probably the most important. It will be the primary key field and will uniquely identify each row.

To Identify a Primary Key Column

The primary key column may now be identified using the BUILD KEY command. The primary key in the **customers** table just created will be the **custid** column.

Type:

```
BUILD KEY FOR custid IN customers
```

This command has identified the column **custid** as the primary key column. You could build keys for other columns as well. Doing so speeds up the query process when searching for unique qualities in a row. For now, you will identify only one column per table.

To Create Additional Tables

Create: additional tables for **salesreps** and **sales,** using the information from Chapter 2 and on the next page.

Concerning the salesreps table:

a. The **repid** column in the **salesreps** table should be constrained as an INTEGER NOT NULL column and identified as the primary key column as well.
b. Make the **repfname** column NOT NULL and allow a width of 20.
c. Use DATE as the type for the **hiredate** column (you do not need to include the width. The format will automatically appear as shown).
d. Use REAL as the type for the **commiss** column. Again, no width is necessary. This width is added for text columns only.

Concerning the sales table:

a. Build a primary key column for the **sales** table using **invid**. Make this column INTEGER and NOT NULL.
b. **Invdate** is a DATE column.
c. **repidid** is an INTEGER and NOT NULL column.
d. **custid** is INTEGER and NOT NULL.
c. **Custid** is INTEGER and NOT NULL.
d. **Netamt** and **tax** are CURRENCY columns.

Note: Do not worry about the data contained in the rows, you are only defining the tables at this time.

repid	repfname	hiredate	commiss
1	Alex Baldwin	11/5/87	.14
2	Judy Marshall	5/4/89	.12
3	Karen Anderson	7/16/88	.13
4	Roger Maltby	3/10/86	.15
5	Morris Crenshaw	10/21/89	.11

Table 2 salesreps

invid	invdate	repid	custid	netamt	tax
111	1/7/90	2	15	$350.00	$28.00
112	1/28/90	1	17	$225.00	$18.00
113	2/15/90	3	12	$90.00	$7.29
114	2/23/90	1	16	$150.00	$12.15
115	2/26/90	4	18	$75.00	$6.08
116	3/1/90	3	19	$175.00	$14.00

Table 3 sales

ALTERING THE STRUCTURE OF A TABLE

Suppose that you have made an error in the structure of your table or simply want to change the table after it has been created. The ALTER TABLE command is not part of the ANSI standard, but it is widely used and has been adopted by R:BASE as one of the standard SQL commands. It enables you to change the definitions of existing tables.

To Add a New Column

In the previous exercise you left off an important column, **totamt** in the **sales** table. It will be added later. Suppose, however, that you have left off a column and would like to add it to one of the tables. The process is listed below.

You would type:

```
ALTER TABLE <table name> ADD <column name>
    CURRENCY
```

Adding a new column in this way always adds it to the end of the table. As when you are creating the table columns for the first time, you could add several columns to a table. In doing so, you would separate column definitions by commas and end the final column definition with a semicolon as in the following syntax example.

Example for adding multiple new columns:

```
ALTER TABLE <table name> ADD <column name> <data
    type> <size>, <column name2> <data type> <size>,
    <column name3> <data type> <size>
```

Other than adding a column, it is usually recommended that you limit your use of the ALTER TABLE command. If you use this command to alter the table extensively after data has been added or after multiple views (discussed in Chapter 8) have been created, the data may be altered.

If a great many changes need to be made in a table immediately after it is created, it is often best to create a new table and delete the original one.

ADDING, DELETING, AND CHANGING VALUES

Now that your tables are created, you can add data values to them. In this exercise, you add rows of data to your tables, remove rows, and change values within the columns on any given row. Three primary commands will be used in these examples: INSERT, UPDATE, and DELETE. These are not actually SQL command words, they are Data Manipulation Language (DML) command words. Don't let this confuse you, however; just focus on the fact that they are often used with SQL commands and relational database systems.

To Enter Values in a Table

Use this command to enter the first three rows of values into each of your three tables. As you are entering the values, you must insert a single quote before and after character values. In the customers table, you had a single INT column for **custid** and all other columns held CHAR values.

1. Type:

   INSERT INTO customers VALUES 11,'Frances Gates','300 Brighton St.','Seattle','WA'

   INSERT INTO customers VALUES 12,'Lloyd Ohlsen','103 First Ave.','Seattle','WA'

2. Continue this procedure until you have inserted the first three lines into each of your tables. The tables are shown for reference.

custid	name	address	city	state
11	Frances Gates	300 Brighton St.	Seattle	WA
12	Lloyd Ohlsen	103 First Avenue	Seattle	WA
13	Yvonne Lewis	1515 N..E. 50th	Kirkland	WA
14	Dale Glenn	2518 25th N.E.	Redmond	WA
15	Robert Hill	15 Union Rd.	Spokane	WA
16	Rachel Cole	1600 Creekside Dr.	Portland	OR
17	Susan Leland	5157 Caribou Ave.	Anchorage	AK
18	Donn Hansen	900 Deep Freeze Ct.	Fairbanks	AK
19	Jean Randolph	101 Mariposa	Fresno	CA
20	Tom Cranston	15 Seneca St.	Oakland	CA

Table 1 customers

repid	repfname	hiredate	commiss
1	Alex Baldwin	11/5/87	.14
2	Judy Marshall	5/4/89	.12
3	Karen Anderson	7/16/88	.13
4	Roger Maltby	3/10/86	.15
5	Morris Crenshaw	10/21/89	.11

Table 2 salesreps

invid	invdate	repid	custid	netamt	tax	totamt
111	1/7/90	2	15	$350.00	$28.00	
112	1/28/90	1	17	$225.00	$18.00	
113	2/15/90	3	12	$90.00	$7.29	
114	2/23/90	1	16	$150.00	$12.15	
115	2/26/90	4	18	$75.00	$6.08	
116	3/1/90	3	19	$175.00	$14.00	

Table 3 sales

About NULL Values

It happens in any database table that sometimes you do not have values for a particular column. Suppose, for example, that you did not have a city for Dale Glenn in the customers table. In that case, you would need to enter a NULL value when adding a row of information.

1. Type:

   INSERT INTO customers VALUES 14,'Dale Glenn','2518 25th N.E.',NULL,'WA'

Note: NULL does not need to be enclosed in quotes it has a special value and is not considered a TEXT value. This command inserts a zero (0) into the TEXT row.

2. Type:

   SELECT * FROM customers

This command selects ALL (*) rows and columns from the table customers. You will probably see only the first four columns on the screen. Not all information is visible. Commands used to view individual columns will be discussed later in this chapter. Anytime it is used as a "wild card," it locates all values. Sometimes the asterisk is used to locate all values within given conditions. You will see numerous variations of this throughout this text. You can now view the NULL value of -0- entered into the city column.

To Replace a NULL Value

You may add a value in place of NULL at any time. Suppose you recently acquired the information about the city in which Dale Glenn lives. It is Redmond.

1. Type:

   UPDATE customers SET city = 'Redmond' WHERE custid = 14

Note: You may use single or double quotation marks. Where both are used, it is easier to use double quote on the outside and single quote on the inside.

2. Type:

   SELECT * FROM customers

to see the change in the table.

In this instruction, you are indicating into which row you would like 'Redmond' to be inserted. You have stated that Redmond should go into the city column of the row of custid 14. The city column is a TEXT type column, and, therefore, Redmond is typed in quotation marks.

To Delete Rows

You can remove rows from a table. The command DELETE FROM removes entire rows from a table. It may also be used to delete all rows from a table and thus empty the table. The next command, DROP TABLE, will tell you how to delete an entire table, which can only be done if all rows are removed.

To view the **salesreps** table:

1. Type:

   SELECT * FROM salesreps

Remove a row from the **salesreps** table by doing the following:

2. Type:

   DELETE FROM salesreps WHERE repid = 3

3. Press: **Enter**

Karen Anderson is now deleted and all column information is deleted as well for the row equal to **repid** = **3**.

Now delete all rows in the **salesreps** table.

1. Type:

   DELETE FROM salesreps

2. Press: **Enter**

3. Press **Enter** again to continue. Note that you have the option of stopping this operation at this time as well.

All rows are now deleted. You will notice that SQL does not display the results of a command on the screen; however, the rows are deleted and you could now apply the DROP TABLE command to remove the entire table.

To Drop a Table

The DROP TABLE command is used to remove a table. It is discussed at this time so that you will have practice in dropping and redoing a table. Normally, the DROP TABLE command cannot be used to get rid of a table containing rows. The procedure for deleting rows was discussed in the step above.

Now drop the **salesreps** table.

1. Type: DROP TABLE salesreps
2. Press: **Enter** to display the message "Press Enter to remove table salesreps"
3. Press: **Enter** to delete the table

To Change Row Values:

The UPDATE command is used to change some of the values in a row. You give the command by using UPDATE and the name of the table that needs some changes. A SET clause indicates the changes that will be made. In this exercise, you will change the values in the table "sales" and then change them back again to the original values. You have several options with the UPDATE command. They are:

* replacing all values in a column by a new value
* replacing the values in selected rows only
* replacing values in more than one column
* using expressions in an UPDATE
* updating NULL values

1. Create the **salesreps** table again and practice inserting the data values as learned earlier. Insert only the first three rows of the table. To get started, use the following syntax:

   CREATE TABLE salesreps repid INTEGER NOT NULL, repfname TEXT(20) NOT NULL, hiredate DATE, commiss REAL

2. Build a key on **repid**.

BUILD KEY FOR repid IN salesreps

3. Add the first three rows of data again. A copy of the table follows.

repid	repfname	hiredate	commiss
1	Alex Baldwin	11/5/87	.14
2	Judy Marshall	5/4/89	.12
3	Karen Anderson	7/16/88	.13
4	Roger Maltby	3/10/86	.15
5	Morris Crenshaw	10/21/89	.11

Table 2 salesreps

To UPDATE all values in a column:

This command will update all values in a column so that they contain the same value.

1. Type:

UPDATE salesreps SET commiss = .15

2. Press: **Enter** to continue

3. Type:

SELECT * FROM salesreps

to view the results.

The commission rate for persons in the first three rows, Baldwin, Marshall, and Anderson, is changed from .14, .12, and .13, respectively, to .15 for each person.

To UPDATE specific rows:

This command will update only specific rows containing one particular value. As an example, let's say that we know that the hiredate of all employees listed as 5/4/89 was actually 5/5/89 because the personnel manager was out on 5/4. The hiredate, therefore, needs to be changed for all persons with a hiredate of 5/4. You know that only one person is in your table with that hiredate; however, this command would work the same if 50 people were hired on 5/4.

1. Type:

    UPDATE salesreps SET hiredate = 5/5/89 WHERE hiredate = 5/4/89

The hiredate of 5/4/89 is replaced throughout the table by the actual hiredate of 5/5/89.

2. View the table now with the SELECT * command. It should be similar to Figure 2.1.

repid	repfname	hiredate	commiss
1	Alex Baldwin	11/05/87	.15
2	Judy Marshall	05/05/89	.15
3	Karen Anderson	07/16/88	.15

Figure 2.1 Results of an UPDATE command

3. Change: the hiredate back to 5/4/89 and view the results with the SELECT command

To UPDATE multiple columns:

So far, you have updated the values in only one column at a time. You have additional flexibility with SQL commands that allow you to update multiple columns. For this exercise, you will change some values in the **sales** table.

In the following steps, you will change the values for a particular customer. This might seem an unlikely string of values to change, but you will understand the ease with which you can adjust certain values in more than one column at a time.

1. Type:

    UPDATE sales SET invid = 117, invdate = 2/20/90, custid = 25 WHERE netamt = 90.00

2. Type:

    SELECT * FROM sales

The results are shown in Figure 2.2

invid	invdate	repid	custid	netamt	tax
111	01/07/90	2	15	$350.00	$28.00
112	01/28/90	1	17	$225.00	$18.00
117	02/20/90	3	25	$90.00	$7.29

Figure 2.2 Changing column data values through the UPDATE command

This set of commands changes the values in the first three columns of the third row in the **sales** table. The SET command changes all values of invid, invdate, and custid to the new values given in the command when it finds a netamt equal to $90.00.

For practice now,

3. Change: the columns back to their original values of 113, 2/15/90, and 12

4. Use the UPDATE command from step 1 to change the values back.

then,

5. Use the INSERT command to insert *all remaining rows* in all three tables. The tables are shown on the following page for reference. Remember to include single quotes around all text columns.

   Example:

   INSERT INTO customers VALUES 11, 'Frances Gates','300 Brighton Street','Seattle','WA'

custid	name	address	city	state
11	Frances Gates	300 Brighton St.	Seattle	WA
12	Lloyd Ohlsen	103 First Avenue	Seattle	WA
13	Yvonne Lewis	1515 N. E. 50th	Kirkland	WA
14	Dale Glenn	2518 25th N.E.	Redmond	WA
15	Robert Hill	15 Union Rd.	Spokane	WA
16	Rachel Cole	1600 Creekside Dr.	Portland	OR
17	Susan Leland	5157 Caribou Ave.	Anchorage	AK
18	Donn Hansen	900 Deep Freeze Ct.	Fairbanks	AK
19	Jean Randolph	101 Mariposa	Fresno	CA
20	Tom Cranston	15 Seneca St.	Oakland	CA

Table 1 customers

repid	repfname	hiredate	commiss
1	Alex Baldwin	11/5/87	.14
2	Judy Marshall	5/4/89	.12
3	Karen Anderson	7/16/88	.13
4	Roger Maltby	3/10/86	.15
5	Morris Crenshaw	10/21/89	.11

Table 2 salesreps

invid	invdate	repid	custid	netamt	tax	totamt
111	1/7/90	2	15	$350.00	$28.00	
112	1/28/90	1	17	$225.00	$18.00	
113	2/15/90	3	12	$90.00	$7.29	
114	2/23/90	1	16	$150.00	$12.15	
115	2/26/90	4	18	$75.00	$6.08	
116	3/1/90	3	19	$175.00	$14.00	

Table 3 sales

To UPDATE with expressions:

It is possible to perform calculations within an expression. This is a useful feature when you need to update all values by a percentage for example. In the following steps, you will calculate the amount of **tax** at .06 percent of **netamt** when the **netamt** is greater than $200.00. Again, you will use the **sales** table.

1. Type:

```
UPDATE sales SET tax = netamt * .06 WHERE netamt >
    200.00
```

The tax has been computed for the first two rows, which contained net amount values of $225.00 and $350.00 as shown in Figure 2.3 and you can view with SELECT * FROM sales.

invid	invdate	repid	custid	netamt	tax
111	01/07/90	2	15	$350.00	$21.00
112	01/28/90	1	17	$225.00	$13.50
113	02/15/90	3	12	$90.00	$7.29
114	02/23/90	1	16	$150.00	$12.15
115	02/26/90	4	18	$75.00	$6.08
116	03/01/90	3	19	$175.00	$14.00

Figure 2.3 UPDATE command with expressions on the **sales** table

The ALTER TABLE command was discussed briefly at the beginning of this chapter. Now is the time to add the **Totamt** column so that the tax and total amount can be computed.

2. Type:

   ALTER TABLE sales ADD totamt currency

Compute the total amount now. Remember that the **Totamt** column was added but has not yet received data values.

2. Type:

   UPDATE sales SET totamt = netamt + tax WHERE netamt > 10.00

Since all net amount values are greater than $10.00, the total will be computed for all rows in the table.

3. View only the totamt column again to see the updated results by typing:

   SELECT totamt FROM sales

The results appear in Figure 2.4.

totamt
$371.00
$238.50
$97.29
$162.15
$81.08
$189.00

Figure 2.4 Results of an UPDATE command

*Note: Typing SELECT * FROM sales would not allow all columns to appear on the screen at one time. You could also select a combination of columns to view, such as netamt, tax, totamt.*

To Change the Output Destination of a Table

Now output your table to the printer or the screen. You can use the OUTPUT command any time you want to view a table or print out the results of a query or table.

1. Type:

   OUTPUT PRINTER

All results will not be printed.

2. Type:

   SELECT * FROM sales

To send all columns from the **sales** table to the printer.

Note: Not all columns will appear (totamt may not show because of the width of the screen). You can view the totamt column by typing SELECT totamt FROM sales.

3. Type:

   OUTPUT SCREEN

to return control of the output to the screen.

4. Type:

   SELECT * FROM sales

You can see the results of this command on the screen.

CHAPTER 5

CREATING INDEXES

PREVIEW

The main purpose of an index is to expedite the search for values within columns. The tables you will encounter in this text are small tables. They are used for convenience and ease in presenting concepts to you. However, most tables created through the use of a database program are extremely large and contain many more columns and perhaps hundreds of rows of data values. If the data were left in the order in which it was originally entered at the keyboard, it would be a collection of numeric and alphabetical values with absolutely no logical order. Because one of the primary purposes of creating tables in the first place is so that you can search through them for particular characteristics and similarities, it is essential that the data be recognized so that searches can be accomplished as quickly as possible. Creating indexes addresses this very problem. Another primary function of indexes is that of forcing values in a column to contain unique values. The system can then quickly locate this unique value as an identifier of a specific row of data.

Look at the customers table again. It contains only a few customers. You can imagine a situation, however, where there might be 50,000 customers for one business, such as a large chain department store. If you requested a search through all customer records for customer number 38,920, the program would have to search every single record until it located the correct number. When an index is created on the customer number column, a specific number may be located immediately.

An index does take up some memory and may slow operations, but on the whole it is a very useful and necessary function of SQL and database programs.

CREATING INDEXES

You can create a single index on one column, such as **custid** in the **customers** table, or on more than one column, such as **custid, name, city.** If you create a single index using more than one column, the result is that the first column is ordered, then the second is ordered within the first, and finally the third within the second, and so on.

You can create as many indexes as you want; however, you might want to create indexes only on the columns you are fairly certain will be frequently accessed when performing queries.

One column that will probably be used frequently to gather information about customers is the **custid** column in the **customers** table. Notice that **custid** is used again in the **sales** table. If the **custid** column is indexed once, it is not necessary to index it again in the **sales** table.

1. Type:

   CREATE INDEX ON customers custid

2. Press: **Enter**

Note: You may use the same name for the index as used for the column. Doing so makes it easier to remember the names of indexes you have created. You may remember that in Chapter 3 you created a primary key on the same column. Ordinarily you would need to use only the BUILD KEY command or the CREATE INDEX command to identify a particular column. You are using the same column this time only for convenience's sake and because you would likely create an index on this unique type of column in actual practice.

The syntax for the command written in step 1 follows this format:

CREATE INDEX ON table name column name

Once an index is created, you are no longer aware of it. When a query is performed and the system is searching for a particular data value, it will apply the index created as it is needed.

3. Create indexes from the **salesreps** table on **repid** and from the **sales** table on **invid**. Use the syntax shown above.

4. Create one more index for the **salesreps** table on the **commiss** column.

To Remove an Index

Normally, you are unaware of the existence of an index. An index is simply accessed when it is needed. You may, however, be aware that you have created many indexes (perhaps one on each column or an ordered index using multiple columns), and later decide you would like to delete some of them because you feel they are rarely used and you would like to remove them from storage.

To remove the index created on the **commiss** column in the **salesreps** table, do the following:

1. Type:

   DROP INDEX commiss IN salesreps

2. Press: **Enter**

The commiss index is deleted.

REINFORCEMENT EXERCISES

RECALL QUESTIONS

1. What is the command used to create a new table?

2. Assume you want the following columns defined in a table, how will the format appear on the screen?

   name
   address
   city
   zip

3. What does the ALTER TABLE command do?

4. Write a sample command to enter a row of values in the columns defined in question 2.

5. How is a NULL value inserted into a row? Give an example.

6. How would you delete a single row from a table? Give an example.

7. What must be done before a table can be dropped?

8. Suppose you wanted to change all N values in the DuesPd column to Y. Write a command that will accomplish this.

9. Write a command that will create an index on a column called ZIP from the **clients** table.

10. What exactly does an index command do? What is its purpose?

PRACTICE EXERCISE 1

1. Create a new database called MEMBER.

2. Create a table for the following club membership list called **cmembers.**

35934	Randle, Colleen	1/2/91	3.25
32954	Jones, Randall	1/3/91	2.95
29575	Wilson, Raymond	1/4/91	3.80
32995	Costner, Jerry	1/5/91	3.00
29788	Mason, Sandra	1/4/91	4.00
27837	Madsen, Olivia	1/3/91	3.00
27857	Petrella, Chris	1/5/91	3.95
27858	Ferrier, Karen	1/4/91	3.50
32789	Jefferson, Peggy	1/3/91	3.60
54717	McRannall, Oren	1/2/91	3.70

3. Decide on appropriate column names, widths, and types.

4. Add data to the table as shown. *Hint*: INSERT INTO **cmembers** VALUES (......)

5. Add a new column called **paid** and insert the following list of values into the column:

Randle	Y
Jones	Y
Wilson	N
Costner	Y
Mason	N
Madsen	Y
Petrella	N
Ferrier	Y
Jackson	Y
McRannall	Y

6. Delete the row for member Olivia Madsen.

7. Change the value N to Y for Petrella.

8. Create an index on the identification number in the first column.

PRACTICE EXERCISE 2

1. Add this table to the database called MEMBERS. Call it the **clients** table and label the columns as follows:

   ID
   Name
   Company
   Address
   City
   State
   Zip

   The ID is the only INTEGER field; all others are character fields.

   Insert NULL values where data is unknown. Create the necessary primary key columns and any NOT NULL columns.

251
Michael Tucker
Software Unlimited
1984 Newton Road
Seattle WA 98102

260
Selena Ho
The Northwest Bank
1900 Wilson Plaza
Bellevue WA 98004

252
Charles Baker
Independent Consultants
19451 N. E. 45th
Seattle WA 98107

270
William Brown
CTech Corporation
2100 Plaza Center
Kirkland WA 98032

256
Bonnie Sills
CTech Corporation
East Hills Branch
Tukwilla WA 98152

263
Robert Long
Long, Lopez, & Tukesburry
9800 Plaza Suite
Bellevue WA 98007

258
Sandra Krogstad
Krogstad and Company
5125 Compton Circle
Woodinville WA 98042

274
Thomas Judd
Software Express Services
North Cromlin Blvd
Issaquah WA 98027

273
Trisha Smith
Julien's Computer Services
North Gilman Square
Issaquah WA 98027

272
Kristal Hodges
The Computer Company
1001 Cromwell Plaza
Seattle WA 98108

271
Douglas Grover
Grover and Associates
123 4th Avenue NE
Seattle WA 98119

264
Nevell Mills
The Baldwin Company
98 Baldwin Place
Seattle WA 98101

253
Theodore Gonzales
The Best Furniture Store
Century Plaza, Suite 201
Bellevue WA 98005

257
Trisha Van der Haven
The Eastside Medical Clinic
1785 118th NE
Bellevue WA 98007

254
Laura Fischer
The Toy Business
2904 20th NW
Kirkland WA (zip is unknown)

261
Wendy Wilson
Wilson's Custom Tailoring
87 Designer Square
Woodinville WA 98043

265
Julien Newnam
Northwest Trekking Services
1400 Forest Road
North Bend WA 98038

259
Patrick Randle
The Delano Charters
1976 Lakewood Way
Seattle WA (zip is unknown)

280
Jim Hill
Silver Swan, Inc.
Southlake Drive
Seattle WA 98104

273
Gill Ackerman
Elegant Tours
East Lake View Drive
Seattle WA 98116

2. Create indexes on the ID, city, and zip.

3. View the tables you have created so far in the MEMBER database, and list the columns in each. Make sure the columns and data types are correct.

Use,

SELECT * FROM tablename

for each of the tables. Remember, you may also look at specific columns by typing, for example, SELECT col1, col2 FROM cmembers or clients.

4. Remove the index for city.

5. Remove the NULL value for client 254 and insert 98032.

6. Remove the NULL value for client 259 and insert 98144.

7. Insert the following new clients:

278
Jacques Thiry
Llama Distributors
Admiralty Drive
Port Townsend WA 98100

276
Hazel Anderton
Buckett O'Pups
104th Avenue
Burien WA 98110

266
Phil Eiler
Resources Ltd.
98 Curiosity Drive
Seattle WA 98101

Send all output to the printer.

ANSWERS TO THE RECALL QUESTIONS

1. CREATE TABLE table name

2. CREATE TABLE new name TEXT(20), address TEXT(25), city TEXT(25), zipcode INTEGER

   This is an example and the length may vary, depending on your widest value in the column.

3. Allows the user to add a column or multiple columns to a table.

4. INSERT INTO table name VALUES('Jane Smith','225 S. Market St.','Seattle',98114)

5. INSERT INTO table name VALUES('Jane Smith','225 S. Market St.','Seattle',NULL)

   It is substituted for an unknown value. Because the type is also unknown, it is not necessary to include the quote marks.

6. DELETE FROM table name WHERE name = 'Jane Smith'

7. All rows must be deleted from it.

8. UPDATE clients SET duespd = Y

9. CREATE INDEX ON clients zip

10. It sorts a column into ascending order for more rapid query performance.

NOTES

PART 3
QUERIES

CHAPTER 6

PERFORMING SINGLE-TABLE QUERIES

PREVIEW

This chapter will explore several ways in which you can draw information out of your tables--commonly called performing queries. This chapter will look at querying a single table at a time. Chapter 7 will explore querying two or more tables for information. One of the major commands you will use is SELECT. It is perhaps one of the most frequently used commands for retrieving information from a table. There are many variations of SELECT; therefore, it will be looked at in detail. In addition to the SELECT command, you can also query your table using special operators such as BETWEEN, LIKE, and NOT; special clauses such as GROUP BY and HAVING; and the ORDER BY expression, which enables you to experience sorting a column of data values. All of these SQL features as well as a few others will be practiced in this chapter.

When a query is performed, the arrangement of the data values in the original table does not change. The information from the query is shown in the form of output on the screen or sometimes is sent to a printer. It is temporary output and is meant for the user's information about what is contained in a table or tables. The use of the SELECT command is amazingly flexible. This single command can be extended to draw out just about any information you may want from a table.

USING THE *SELECT* COMMAND

The SELECT command is used to draw simple to detailed information out of your SQL tables. Before beginning, it is good to have tables of a reasonably large enough size that the information gathered from a SELECT command is meaningful. So it will be necessary for you to add additional rows to your three tables.

1. Be sure you have added the remaining rows to your tables. The procedure for adding rows is discussed in Chapter 4. The tables from Chapter 2 follow and contain all of the rows you should have in your finished tables before continuing in this chapter.

2. Be sure the MASTER database is open.

custid	fname	address	city	state
11	Frances Gates	300 Brighton St.	Seattle	WA
12	Lloyd Ohlsen	103 First Avenue	Seattle	WA
13	Yvonne Lewis	1515 N. E. 50th	Kirkland	WA
14	Dale Glenn	2518 25th N.E.	Redmond	WA
15	Robert Hill	15 Union Rd.	Spokane	WA
16	Rachel Cole	1600 Creekside Dr.	Portland	OR
17	Susan Leland	5157 Caribou Ave.	Anchorage	AK
18	Donn Hansen	900 Deep Freeze Ct.	Fairbanks	AK
19	Jean Randolph	101 Mariposa	Fresno	CA
20	Tom Cranston	15 Seneca St.	Oakland	CA

Table 1 **customers**

repid	repfname	hiredate	commiss
1	Alex Baldwin	11/5/87	.15
2	Judy Marshall	5/4/89	.15
3	Karen Anderson	7/16/88	.15
4	Roger Maltby	3/10/86	.15
5	Morris Crenshaw	10/21/89	.11

Table 2 **salesreps**

invid	invdate	repid	custid	netamt	tax	totamt
111	1/7/90	2	15	$350.00	$21.00	$371.00
112	1/28/90	1	17	$225.00	$13.50	$238.50
113	2/15/90	3	12	$90.00	$7.29	$97.29
114	2/23/90	1	16	$150.00	$12.15	$162.15
115	2/26/90	4	18	$75.00	$6.08	$81.08
116	3/1/90	3	19	$175.00	$14.00	$189.00

Table 3 **sales**

To Retrieve Specific Columns

In its very simplest form, you can draw information from a table using the following brief SELECT command.

Type:

SELECT custid, fname, state FROM customers

The output shows a list of the columns **custid**, **fname**, and **state** from the table **customers**,as shown below in Figure 3-1.

custid	fname	state
11	Frances Gates	WA
12	Lloyd Ohlsen	WA
13	Yvonne Lewis	WA
14	Dale Glenn	WA
15	Robert Hill	WA
16	Rachel Cole	OR
17	Susan Leland	AK
18	Donn Hansen	AK
19	Jean Randolph	CA
20	Tom Cranston	CA

Figure 3.1 Results of retrieving specific columns

Because no special conditions were asked for in the command (only the selected column names), all data values in those columns are shown.

To Retrieve All Columns

You have already practiced using the SELECT command to view all columns in a table. View the columns in the **customers** table.

Type:

```
SELECT * FROM customers
```

This simple command asks for all rows and columns with the use of the asterisk (*).

To Retrieve Columns in a Specific Order

With the use of the two commands just completed, the columns were retrieved in the order in which you originally defined them in the table. If you do not give special instructions to have them appear otherwise, they will always appear in the order in which they were defined. You do, however, have the option of reordering them for different viewing. Continuing with the **customers** table, try the following.

Type:

```
SELECT state,fname,custid FROM customers
```

Now a list is produced showing the columns reordered with state appearing first, then name, and last custid.

USING THE *DISTINCT* ARGUMENT

Although the tables you are working with are small, they contain some redundant values. For example, look at the **sales** table. This table includes information about which sales representatives made sales for a given period of time. In a real-life situation, this kind of table might contain hundreds of entries and the **repid** column might contain the numbers 1, 2, or 3 repeated many times for each sale made by a particular sales representative. This small table can, however, be used as an example of getting rid of redundant data in output.

Suppose for example, that all you wanted to know was which representatives made sales during this period. You could locate this information in one of two ways.

1. Type:

```
SELECT repid FROM sales
```

A list is produced of all id's in the **repid** column. Notice that repid numbers one and three are repeated. If they appear more than once in the table, they will appear more than once in the output. This is okay when a table is small, but suppose that all you really needed to know was which representatives made sales and not how many times they made them. You could,

2. Type:

```
SELECT DISTINCT repid FROM sales
```

This time a list is retrieved of only the distinct repids, and multiple occurrences of repids are not shown.

USING THE *WHERE* CLAUSE

The WHERE clause uses comparison operators to look for conditions in a table or tables. The operators which may be used are shown in Table 3.1.

Operator	Meaning
=	Equal to
<	Less than
>	Greater than
<=	Less than or equal to
>=	Greater than or equal to
<>	Not equal to

Table 3.1 Comparison operators

The WHERE clause allows you to use the SELECT command to define a condition that is either true or false for any row in your table. When the output is shown, it contains only the information for which the condition is true.

1. Type:

SELECT invid, netamt FROM sales WHERE netamt > 200.00

The results of this command are that all rows containing conditions of net amounts greater than 200.00 are shown. Shown also is the invoice id number (invid). This is a simple WHERE clause. WHERE clauses are constructed using the SELECT-FROM-WHERE format. Your screen should look similar to that shown in Figure 3.2.

invid	netamt
111	$350.00
112	$225.00

Figure 3.2 Results of using the WHERE clause

If you wanted to view all columns in rows containing amounts greater than 200.00, you would:

2. Type:

SELECT * FROM sales WHERE netamt > 200.00

*Note: Once again, your screen may not display all of the columns. This will continue to happen with tables containing as many columns as the sales table or the customers table. You will need to remember to select specific column names if you want to see columns other than those displayed through the SELECT * command.*

To Apply Compound Conditions

Compound conditions are those that look for more than one existing condition in a table. In the previous examples, you were looking for a single condition within the rows of a table. In the following examples, you will look for multiple conditions. Compound conditions use the connectors AND, OR, and NOT. They are defined as stated in Table 3.2.

AND	Two simple conditions are connected by the word AND. In this case, both the condition on the left and the condition on the right must be true.
OR	Two simple conditions are connected by the word OR. In this case, either the condition on the left or the condition on the right can be true.
NOT	When NOT precedes a condition, the reverse is true. Put another way, if the original condition is true, the new condition will be false; if the original condition is false, the new condition will be true.

Table 3.2 Compound Conditions

Working from the sales table again, look for the compound condition of the representatives who sold less than 100.00 during February and March. Display the columns for total amount and the representatives identification number.

1. Type:

```
SELECT repid, totamt FROM sales WHERE totamt < 100.00
    AND invdate >= 2/1/90
```

This command produces the display of repid and totamt for representatives 3 and 4, who both sold under 100.00 through February and March, as shown in Figure 3.3.

```
repid           totamt
--------------- ---------------
              3          $97.29
              4          $81.08
```

Figure 3.3 Results of a compound condition on the **sales** table

Now look for one condition or the other in a table.

2. Type:

```
SELECT totamt, invid, invdate FROM sales WHERE totamt >
    300.00 OR custid = 20
```

This will produce a list of one condition or the other. Your output shows one row with a total amount of 371.00, as shown in Figure 3.4.

This is the only condition that existed because there were no rows with a customer identification number of 20. If both conditions had existed, both would have been pulled out.

totamt	invid	invdate
$371.00	111	01/07/90

Figure 3.4 Results of a compound condition on the **sales** table

You could also search for rows that do not contain a particular condition, such as all sales except those where repid = 1.

3. Type:

```
SELECT invid, repid, totamt FROM sales WHERE NOT repid
    = 1
```

This command produces a list of all representatives who are not representatives number 1, as shown in Figure 3.5.

invid	repid	totamt
111	2	$371.00
113	3	$97.29
115	4	$81.08
116	3	$189.00

Figure 3.5 Results of a compound condition on the **sales** table

USING THE *BETWEEN* OPERATOR

Suppose you wanted to retrieve a group of numbers between two values. In this example, you will retrieve a range of values from the totamt column in the sales table that range between the values of 150.00 and 250.00.

1. Type:

```
SELECT invid, custid, totamt FROM sales WHERE totamt
    BETWEEN 150.00 AND 250.00
```

The result produces the table shown in Figure 3.6, which contains invids 112 , 114, and 116 that are within our range.

invid	custid	totamt
112	17	$238.50
114	16	$162.15
116	19	$189.00

Figure 3.6 Results of a BETWEEN operator on the **sales** table

USING THE *LIKE* OPERATOR

The LIKE command is applied only to TEXT data types. Two types of wild cards can be used with the LIKE command:

* The underscore character (_) stands for a missing character. You would use the underscore character if you wanted to search for all words beginning with one character and ending with another. For instance, if you wanted to search for all words beginning with s and ending in t, you would write 's_t'. This would match all such words as 'sit' and 'sat'.

* The % sign is probably the most frequently used of the wild cards. It stands for a series of numbers or characters. If you are searching for all words containing 'st%c%' for example, you would match 'stick', 'stock', and so on.

1. Locate all customers from the **customers** table who live in cities beginning with S and display all columns in the result.

2. Type:

```
SELECT * FROM customers WHERE city LIKE 'S%'
```

This command selects all columns from the customers table and, with the use of the LIKE operator and the wild card, locates all cities beginning with S, in this case Seattle and Spokane, Washington, as shown in Figure 3.7.

custid	fname	address	city
11	Frances Gates	300 Brighton St.	Seattle
12	Lloyd Ohlsen	103 First Avenue	Seattle
15	Robert Hill	15 Union Rd.	Spokane

Figure 3.7 Results of a LIKE operator on the **customers** table

3. Type:

   SELECT * FROM customers WHERE address LIKE '2%'

This command selects customer 14, Dale Glenn.

In both of the examples above, the % indicates a data value that has a match of the initial character of S or the initial figure of 2. No matter what the length of the value in the column, the answer will show all data values, such as the entire address for Dale Glenn.

USING THE *IN* OPERATOR

The IN operator allows you to find particular values without writing lengthy commands. As an example, look at the following command with which you want to locate all customers living in Kirkland, Redmond, or Eugene. Even though Eugene is not one of the cities in the table, you are searching for a possibility of cities within your table, so one of the conditions will be met.

```
SELECT * FROM customers WHERE city = 'Kirkland' OR city
     = 'Redmond' OR city = 'Eugene'
```

You can see that if you were looking for customers in many different cities, a command like this one could become lengthy very quickly.

The command could be written more quickly by using the IN operator when groups of possible conditions for which you are searching are grouped together in a single line command.

Type:

```
SELECT * FROM customers WHERE city IN ('Kirkland',
     'Redmond', 'Eugene')
```

The explicit set of values is written in parentheses, each of the members of the set is enclosed in single quotes, and the members are separated by commas. This is much faster than writing out each set individually and produces the same results as shown in Figure 3.8.

custid	fname	address	city
13	Yvonne Lewis	1515 N.E. 50th	Kirkland
14	Dale Glenn	2518 25th N.E.	Redmond

Figure 3.8 Results of the IN operator on the **customers** table

USING THE *GROUP BY AND ORDER BY* CLAUSES

You can order one column as a subset of another and apply an aggregate (SUM, MAX, MIN, etc.) function to the subset. For example, suppose you wanted to find the greatest total amount achieved by each representative in the **sales** table. Rather than perform a separate query for each representative, you could locate the information in a single GROUP BY clause.

1. Type:

   SELECT repid, MAX(totamt) FROM sales GROUP BY repid

This command displays the **repid** and the maximum or highest value for each representative in the **sales** table. You could type this command with or without the parentheses; however, in this text parentheses will be displayed for easier proofing and previewing of associations. The command MAX must appear in CAPS. The result is grouped on **repid** in ascending order, as shown in Figure 3.9.

repid	max (totamt)
1	$238.50
2	$371.00
3	$189.00
4	$81.08

Figure 3.9 Results of a MAX and GROUP BY clauses on **sales** table

You could also perform calculations within a GROUP BY clause. Suppose you wanted to sum the totamt and group according to the repid.

2. Type:

   SELECT repid, SUM(totamt) FROM sales GROUP BY repid

This command produces a list of repid, netamt and the computed total amount from the **sales** table. It is grouped by repid, with repid ordered in ascending order as shown in Figure 3.10.

repid	sum(totamt)
1	$400.65
2	$371.00
3	$286.29
4	$81.08

Figure 3.10 Results of the GROUP BY clause

You can also produce a listing using the ORDER BY clause that shows selected columns from a table.

3. Type:

```
SELECT netamt, tax, totamt FROM sales ORDER BY repid
```

The results appear in Figure 3.11.

netamt	tax	totamt
$225.00	$13.50	$238.50
$150.00	$12.15	$162.15
$350.00	$21.00	$371.00
$90.00	$7.29	$97.29
$175.00	$14.00	$189.00
$75.00	$6.08	$81.08

Figure 3.11 Results of the ORDER BY Clause

USING THE *HAVING* CLAUSE

When you group by numbers, you cannot use a WHERE clause at the same time. Suppose, for example, that you wanted to search in your sales table for total amounts that are greater than 200.00 and group them by invoice date. In a regular WHERE clause operation, the search is performed a single row at a time and does not recognize groupings. The clause that can handle this operation is the HAVING clause.

1. Type:

```
SELECT invdate, MAX(totamt) FROM sales GROUP BY
    invdate HAVING MAX(totamt) > 200.00
```

This will produce the results of invdate in ascending order and the total amounts over 200.00 as shown in Figure 3.12.

invdate	max(totamt)
01/07/90	$371.00
01/28/90	$238.50

Figure 3.12 Results of using the HAVING clause

REINFORCEMENT EXERCISES

RECALL QUESTIONS

1. What is the purpose of the SELECT command?

2. Write a simple command for retrieving all rows from a particular file. Use any table name.

3. Write a simple command to retrieve the columns name, city, and state from a table called **clients**.

4. What is the major function of the WHERE clause? How does the WHERE clause differ from the HAVING clause?

5. Write a command that will retrieve the columns **name** and **amt** from the table **dues** for all amounts equal to 15.00 with a date of 8/30/90.

6. What does the BETWEEN operator do?

7. How is the LIKE operator used? Give an example.

8. What is the advantage of using the IN operator?

9. What is the difference between a GROUP BY and an ORDER BY clause?

10. Write a sample HAVING command that will retrieve the MAX grade from the **student** table and group by name for all scores greater than 75.

PRACTICE EXERCISE 3

1. Create a database called BOATS and the following table called **charter**. You will be using the BOATS database for more practice exercises in this text.

   Decide appropriate column widths. All columns are integer with the exception of the boat name, registration number, the captain's name, and license.

Boat Name	Reg No.	Captain	No. of Pass.	License	Length	Tonnage	Beam	Speed
Delano	WN6655L	P. J. Randle	6	I	33	9	10	7.5
Irish Mist	WN7256L	J. Paton	49	L O C	56	24	22	10
Spirit O'Sea	WN 6291L	G. Ackerman	225	L O C	130	74	34	14
Sunrise	WN2951R	J. Thiry	29	L O C	74	28	22	7.0
Emrok	WN3251J	L. Crabtree	6	I	43	26	14	8.0
Spirit of Eagle Harbor	WN4512R	R. Burke	49	L I C	62	29	24	11.5
Jack's Ship	WN3200S	J. Kennedy	6	I	28	8	8	6.5
Easy Days	WN2291	R. Smith	6	I	28	8	8	6.0
Elegance	WN7210S	J. Hill	150	L O C	90	60	28	11.5
Just Right	WN2301R	J. Wilson	30	L O	74	26	23	8.0
Time Off	WN2911L	S. Smithson	10	L I	28	8	8.5	6.5
Bill's Barge	WN3410L	W. Winkles	150	L I C	90	60	28	12.0
Joan's Delight	WN5891Q	J. Luckmann	50	L I C	62	30	24	11.5
Pat's Place	WN2578L	P. MacRannall	49	L I C	74	26	23	8.0
The Chip II	WN7891R	S. Wilson	30	L O	70	24	20	6.0

2. Retrieve a list of all boats that can carry more than 100 passengers.

3. Retrieve a list of all boats that are licensed for oceangoing cruises and can cater meals. List the names of the boats, the type of license held, and the number of passengers she can carry. The codes in the license category are:

I	Inland waters
L	Liquor license
O	Ocean
C	Catered meals

4. Query the table for all boats that carry 50 or fewer passengers and are licensed for inland waters only. List the name of the boat, the boat's captain, the length of the vessel, and the license it carries--in that order.

5. Retrieve a listing of all boats with a cruising speed between 6.0 and 8.0. List each boat's name and length.

6. Query the table for all boats with a length of 90 feet or more. Produce a listing of the boats grouped by boat name and show each boat's name and length in the output.

7. Use a HAVING command to retrieve the MAX speed from this table and group by boat name for all speeds greater than 10 knots. Show boat name and speed.

ANSWERS TO THE RECALL QUESTIONS

1. The SELECT command is used to draw information from one or more tables--called querying a table.

2. SELECT * FROM customers

3. SELECT name, city, state FROM clients

4. The major function of a WHERE clause is to define a condition that is either true or false for any row in a table. This is different from HAVING because HAVING is a substitute for WHERE when using GROUP BY or ORDER BY.

5. SELECT name, amt FROM dues WHERE amt = 15.00 AND date = 8/30/90

6. The BETWEEN operator locates amounts between two values, such as between 500.00 and 600.00.

7. The LIKE operator is a wild card operator that searches for conditions unknown by the user. As an example,

   SELECT * FROM sales WHERE name LIKE 'Sm_th%'

   This command would locate all persons with names spelled either Smith or Smyth.

8. The IN operator allows the user to query for multiple conditions without writing out entire command lines for each single condition.

9. The GROUP BY clause groups by one column and then another. The ORDER BY clause sorts a column in ascending order.

10. SELECT name, MAX(grade) FROM student GROUP BY name HAVING MAX(grade) > 75

CHAPTER 7
PERFORMING MULTI-TABLE QUERIES

PREVIEW

In Chapter 6, you learned many ways to query a single table. It is possible to use SQL commands to query multiple tables at the same time. In this chapter you explore joining tables together. This is an extremely useful operation because it shows you the relationship between various columns in a table. You will also experience using the IN and EXIST commands, working with nested queries, using an ALIAS, and working with SET operators.

JOINING TABLES

Probably the most powerful feature of any relational database program is its ability to recognize relationships between multiple tables. That is, in fact, what defines a relational database system. To recognize relationships effectively between two or more tables, variations of the SELECT command are implemented. Using the SELECT command you are able to make connections between numerous tables that would otherwise remain independent, separate entities.

At this time, you have several tables you have created in both the instructional part of this text and the reinforcement exercises. In this chapter and throughout the remainder of the text, you use the original three tables you created in Part 2: **customers**, **salesreps**, and **sales**.

Table and Column Names

Column names are usually recognized as those that you originally assigned when first creating the table, for example, in the **customer** table, the column names are referred to as **custid**, **name**, **address**, and so forth. In fact, the full name of any column is actually the table name *and* the column name separated by a period, as in the examples below from the **customer** table.

customer.custid
customer.name
customer.address

When querying a single table, you do not need to use the table name within the query command. Within individual tables, column names are unique. In this way, querying is kept simple. However, if you look at the following tables, you will see that some of the column names are repeated from table to table. **Repid** is used in both the **sales** table and the **salesreps** table. **Custid** is also repeated. The table name would need to be used in any query including two or more tables with the same column names.

custid	name	address	city	state
11	Frances Gates	300 Brighton St.	Seattle	WA
12	Lloyd Ohlsen	103 First Avenue	Seattle	WA
13	Yvonne Lewis	1515 N. E. 50th	Kirkland	WA
14	Dale Glenn	2518 25th N.E.	Redmond	WA
15	Robert Hill	15 Union Rd.	Spokane	WA
16	Rachel Cole	1600 Creekside Dr.	Portland	OR
17	Susan Leland	5157 Caribou Ave.	Anchorage	AK
18	Donn Hansen	900 Deep Freeze Ct.	Fairbanks	AK
19	Jean Randolph	101 Mariposa	Fresno	CA
20	Tom Cranston	15 Seneca St.	Oakland	CA

Table 1 **customers**

repid	repfname	hiredate	commiss
1	Alex Baldwin	11/5/87	.14
2	Judy Marshall	5/4/89	.12
3	Karen Anderson	7/16/88	.13
4	Roger Maltby	3/10/86	.15
5	Morris Crenshaw	10/21/89	.11

Table 2 **salesreps**

invid	invdate	repid	custid	netamt	tax	totamt
111	1/7/90	2	15	$350.00	$21.00	$371.00
112	1/28/90	1	17	$225.00	$13.50	$238.50
113	2/15/90	3	12	$90.00	$7.29	$97.29
114	2/23/90	1	16	$150.00	$12.15	$162.15
115	2/26/90	4	18	$75.00	$6.08	$81.08
116	3/1/90	3	19	$175.00	$14.00	$189.00

Table 3 **sales**

Adding an extra column:

Before continuing, you are going to add a column to the **salesreps** table. The steps for adding a column were covered in Part 2 and are repeated here for convenience. When you add the new column, it will contain NULL values for all rows in the table. You will then need to replace the NULL values (also covered in the following steps).

1. Type:

```
ALTER TABLE salesreps ADD city TEXT(15)
```

The new column has been added.

Replacing the NULL values:

Use the UPDATE command to add values to the new column.

2. Type:

```
UPDATE salesreps SET city = 'Fresno' WHERE repid = 1

UPDATE salesreps SET city = 'Fairbanks' WHERE repid = 2
```

3. Continue writing UPDATE commands for each of the next three representatives: repid 3, 4, and 5 as follows:

repid	
3	Seattle
4	Spokane
5	Portland

The output is shown below in Figure 3.13.

repid	repfname	hiredate	commiss	city
1	Alex Baldwin	11/05/87	0.15	Fresno
2	Judy Marshall	05/04/89	0.15	Fairbanks
3	Karen Anderson	07/16/88	0.15	Seattle
4	Roger Maltby	03/10/86	0.15	Spokane
5	Morris Crenshaw	10/21/89	0.11	Portland

Figure 3.13 Result of adding a column to **salesreps** table

To Join Two Tables

You now have two tables that contain the column name **city**. Suppose you wanted to join the two tables so that you could see which representatives lived in or near cities in which customers also live.

Type:

```
SELECT customers.fname, salesreps.repfname, salesreps.city
    FROM customers, salesreps WHERE salesreps.city =
    customers.city
```

The table name is necessary only when the column name is the same in both tables; however, for ease of use and for consistency, the examples in this text will include the prefix every time a join is performed.

The previous command drew information from both the **customers** table and the **salesreps** table (thus joining values from both) and displayed the columns of **name** (customer's name), **repfname** (representative's name), and the common cities for each occurrence where the city was the same. The result is shown in Figure 3.14.

customers.fname	salesreps.fname	salesreps.city
Jean Randolph	Alex Baldwin	Fresno
Donn Hansen	Judy Marshall	Fairbanks
Frances Gates	Karen Anderson	Seattle
Lloyd Ohlsen	Karen Anderson	Seattle
Robert Hill	Roger Maltby	Spokane
Rachel Cole	Morris Crenshaw	Portland

Figure 3.14 Results of joining the two tables

To Join More Than Two Tables:

You can also join more than two tables. Suppose for example that you wanted to query all three tables for the city, customer name, and customer ID that made sales from January through March.

Type:

```
SELECT customers.fname, sales.custid, salesreps.city,
    sales.totamt FROM customers, salesreps, sales WHERE
    customers.city = salesreps.city AND customers.custid =
    sales.custid
```

In this command you displayed information from all three tables as stated in the FROM command. You joined the tables by selecting columns from the **customers** table, the **sales** table, and the **salesreps** table. In addition, you matched conditions through the WHERE clause when the cities were the same in the **customers** table and the **salesreps** table and when the customer IDs matched in both the **customers** table and the **sales** table. The results of this join are shown in Figure 3.15.

customers.fname	sales.cust	salesreps.city	sales.totamt
Robert Hill	15	Spokane	$371.00
Lloyd Ohlsen	12	Seattle	$97.29
Rachel Cole	16	Portland	$162.15
Donn Hansen	18	Fairbanks	$81.08
Jean Randolph	19	Fresno	$189.00

Figure 3.15 Results of a multiple table join

USING AN ALIAS

An alias is created when you want to join a table with itself. This is another form of the JOIN command in that it also joins one table to another. This time, however, you are joining a table to itself. This is a useful command for comparing values of rows containing common field values, such as a common **city** in the **customer** table or a common **repid** in the **sales** table. SQL joins the tables only for as long as you are querying information by assigning an alias to a table. It is a temporary command.

To create an alias table, you define the original table and the alias in the FROM command. You also list all columns in the SELECT command.

Type:

```
SELECT first.city, second.city, first.fname FROM customers
    first, salesreps second WHERE first.city = second.city
```

The results are shown in Figure 3.16.

first.city	second.city	first.fname
Fresno	Fresno	Jean Randolph
Fairbanks	Fairbanks	Donn Hansen
Seattle	Seattle	Frances Gates
Seattle	Seattle	Lloyd Ohlsen
Spokane	Spokane	Robert Hill
Portland	Portland	Rachel Cole

Figure 3.16 Results of using an ALIAS

This command looks for the city in the first table, the city in the second table and the name in the first table. The "join" of the table is performed with the FROM command. This line is where SQL creates an alias for the table and joins it to itself. Remember that this action is just temporary while you are performing the query. Information is shown where the cities are the same or a match is found from both tables.

PERFORMING SUBQUERIES

Another feature of SQL commands is the subquery. This is an example of a "nested" query, where one search is performed within another. Generally, when you are using subqueries, you are generating certain values with the inner query that will be tested with the outer query.

To Use a Subquery Command

As an example of a simple nested query, suppose you knew some of the information you wanted from a table, but not other information. Suppose, for example, that you knew the customer identification number of a customer in the **sales** table, but not the name. You could search for that information with the following command.

1. Type:

```
SELECT * FROM customers WHERE custid IN (SELECT
    custid FROM sales WHERE totamt < 200.00)
```

SQL first must evaluate the inner query. As you can see, it is searching the **sales** table for totamt less than 200.00. This searched is based on the **custid** column. After knowing this information, the outer query is then completed by selecting all columns from the **customers** table where the **custid** matches those in the inner query. The result appears in Figure 3.17.

custid	fname	address	city
12	Lloyd Ohlsen	103 First Avenue	Seattle
16	Rachel Cole	1600 Creekside Dr.	Portland
18	Donn Hansen	900 Deep Freeze Ct.	Fairbanks
19	Jean Randolph	101 Mariposa	Fresno

Figure 3.17 Results of a subquery

To Use IN with a Subquery

The IN operator is used with a subquery command to produce any number of rows. Remember that the IN operator is used to define a set of values that match a stated condition. Suppose you wanted to locate all sales made by representatives in Seattle. You could use the IN operator to located all the sales made from the **sales** table by those representatives living in Seattle.

Type:

```
SELECT * FROM sales WHERE repid IN (SELECT repid
  FROM salesreps WHERE city = 'Seattle')
```

In this example, you have the results you wanted. The representative from Seattle was located in the subquery where a search of the **salesreps** table took place. With the **repid** matched to the **city** in the inner query, the outer query displayed all rows from the **sales** table where the **repid** matched that of the **salesreps** table. The results are shown in Figure 3.18.

invid	invdate	repid	custid	netamt	tax
---------	---------	---------	---------	---------	---------
113	02/15/90	3	12	$90.00	$7.29
116	03/01/90	3	19	$175.00	$14.00

Figure 3.18 Results of IN with a Subquery

Note: You may look at totamt separately if desired.

In any of the subquery routines, you do not see the results of the subquery. In the example shown, the equal operator was used because it was known ahead of time that the result would be output of one row of values only. If you feel that the output may be more than one row, you could use any other operator such as greater than, less than, etc.

USING THE *EXISTS* OPERATOR

The EXISTS operator produces a Boolean expression--a true or false value. Some Boolean operators with which you are familiar are AND, OR, and NOT. As with any Boolean expression, you are writing a command that will evaluate values and produce a "true" condition if the values exist and a "false" condition if they do not. This is essentially what the inner loop of the following SELECT command does. When the WHERE EXISTS clause is included, the inner loop will first look for a true condition. If a true condition is located, it will then display the results of the outer loop.

In the following example, you will search the **customers** table for all customers living in Alaska (AK). As you can see before beginning to type the command, you could locate this information more quickly using a simple WHERE command. The EXISTS operator is more efficient when used with the correlated subqueries that follow. This first step, however, shows you the first query routine within the outer query and how the two are related.

Type:

```
SELECT DISTINCT fname, address, city FROM customers
    WHERE EXISTS (SELECT * FROM customers WHERE
    state = 'AK')
```

DISTINCT allows only those unique rows to be displayed. In this example, there are not many duplicate rows to worry about; however, if you were listing all repids and some were duplicated, the DISTINCT command would show only the unique repids and would not duplicate any appearing more than once.

The inner query locates some true conditions. Yes, there are some customers from the state of AK (Alaska). The result is asked for in the outer loop. In this command, you have asked for the name, address, and city of all customers if a true condition is found. The results are displayed in Figure 3.19.

fname	address	city
Dale Glenn	2518 25th N.E.	Kirkland
Donn Hansen	900 Deep Freeze Ct.	Fairbanks
Frances Gates	300 Brighton St.	Seattle
Jean Randolph	101 Mariposa	Fresno
Lloyd Ohlsen	103 First Avenue	Seattle
Rachel Cole	1600 Creekside Dr.	Portland
Robert Hill	15 Union Rd.	Spokane
Susan Leland	5157 Caribou Ave.	Anchorage
Tom Cranston	15 Seneca St.	Oakland
Yvonne Lewis	1515 N.E. 50th	Kirkland

Figure 3.19 Results using the EXISTS operator

To Use EXISTS with Correlated Subqueries

In a correlated subquery, each row is evaluated separately when referenced in the outer query. With this command, you can generate different answers for each row of the table addressed in the outer or main query. The DISTINCT clause also allows for the row information to be unique. If it were not used in the following command, you would achieve output results showing rows for every transaction, rather than grouped.

In the following command, you are querying for representatives who had multiple customers in the **sales** table.

Type:

```
SELECT DISTINCT repid FROM sales outer WHERE EXISTS
    (SELECT * FROM sales inner WHERE inner.repid =
    outer.repid AND inner.custid <> outer.custid)
```

Each time a pass is made through the inner query it locates rows that match the repid value in the outer query, but do not match the custid value (the WHERE clause and the AND Boolean expression, respectively). If rows are found in the inner query that contain an unmatched value, then it implies that there are two different customers for a single sales representative. The results display only two repids as shown in Figure 3.20.

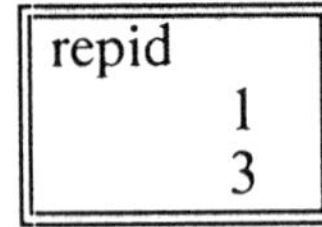

repid
1
3

Figure 3.20 Results of using EXISTS with subqueries.

USING *ANY* OR *SOME*

ANY or SOME are special operators used interchangeably. You can substitute ANY for SOME and vice versa. For the examples in this text, you will see ANY being used. Feel free to use whichever operator seems most comfortable for you.

The ANY operator looks at values produced in a subquery that are true. In the ANY queries, the subquery must select values of the same type as those in the main query, as in the example below.

Type:

```
SELECT * FROM customers WHERE city = ANY (SELECT
    city FROM salesreps)
```

Your output shows the results of the subquery--all city values in the salesreps table--and evaluates to a true condition if any of the city values are equal to the city values in the outer query. So, as you can see, the inner query has an effect on the results of the outer query in that they must match the same values. Remember that in the EXISTS operator, the subquery and the outer query did not need to be the same, and the EXISTS operator simply determines whether or not a subquery produced results. The results of this query are shown in Figure 3.21.

custid	fname	address	city
11	Frances Gates	300 Brighton St.	Seattle
12	Lloyd Ohlsen	103 First Avenue	Seattle
15	Robert Hill	15 Union Rd.	Spokane
16	Rachel Cole	1600 Creekside Dr.	Portland
18	Donn Hansen	900 Deep Freeze Ct.	Fairbanks
19	Jean Randolph	101 Mariposa	Fresno

Figure 3.21 Results of the ANY or SOME operators

USING *ALL*

When using an ALL operator, every value of the subquery must satisfy the condition of the outer query.

Type:

```
SELECT * FROM salesreps WHERE commiss > ALL
    (SELECT commiss FROM salesreps WHERE city =
    'Portland')
```

In this command, the inner loop is locating all sales representatives from Portland with commissions. The true condition was located (one representative is from Portland). The outer query then found all commissions that were higher than that of the Portland representative. The results appear in Figure 3.22.

repid	repfname	hiredate	commiss	city
1	Alex Baldwin	11/05/87	0.15	Fresno
2	Judy Marshall	05/04/89	0.15	Fairbanks
3	Karen Anderson	07/16/88	0.15	Seattle
4	Roger Maltby	03/10/86	0.15	Spokane

Figure 3.22 Results of using the ALL operator

SUMMARY

You have practiced many variations of queries using single and multiple tables. The secret of using these queries successfully is to practice them and experiment with your own variations of the examples presented here. Queries are usually the primary operation of any relational database system. Now that you have had practice with them, you have tackled the primary objective in understanding and working with SQL.

REINFORCEMENT EXERCISES

RECALL QUESTIONS

1. Briefly describe the concept of joining two or more tables.

2. Write a simple join command to display the columns **name** and **city** from a table called **authors** and a table called **publishers**.

3. Write a command to join three tables: **authors**, **publishers**, and **critics**. Display the columns, **aname**, **pname**, **cname**, and **city**. Query for those located in the same cities and where columns **authid** and **pubid** are the same.

4. What is an ALIAS? How is it used?

5. What does a subquery do?

6. How is EXISTS within a correlated subquery the most effective use of this operator?

7. What is the main requirement of the ANY operator?

8. What is the main requirement of the ALL operator?

PRACTICE EXERCISE 4

In this exercise, you will use the table from Practice Exercise 3, **charter**, and will create the tables shown below as well.

1. Create the table shown in the following box. Call it **fuel**.

Boat Name	Length of Boat/Feet	Gallons per Hour/$1 per gallon
Delano	33	1.5
Irish Mist	56	4
Spirit O'Sea	130	17
Sunrise	74	14
Emrok	43	3
Spirit of Eagle Harbor	62	5
Jack's Ship	28	1.0
Easy Days	28	1.0
Elegance	90	8
Just Right	74	13
Time Off	28	2.0
Bill's Barge	90	20
Joan's Delight	62	6
Pat's Place	74	13
The Chip II	70	15

2. Create the table shown in the following box, calling it **crew**.

Boat Name	Captain	Deck Hands	Captain's Wage	Deck Hand Wage
Delano	P. Randle	0	15.00	
Irish Mist	J. Paton	2	15.00	5.00
Spirit O'Sea	G. Ackerman	8	16.00	5.00
Sunrise	J. Thiry	0	15.00	
Emrok	L. Crabtree	1	15.00	5.00
Spirit of Eagle Harbor	R. Burke	2	15.00	5.00
Jack's Ship	J. Kennedy	0	15.00	
Easy Days	R. Smith	1	10.00	5.00
Elegance	J. Hill	7	15.00	5.00
Just Right	J. Wilson	5	15.00	5.00
Time Off	S. Smithson	1	15.00	5.00
Bill's Barge	W. Winkles	2	15.00	5.00
Joan's Delight	J. Luckmann	1	10.00	5.00
Pat's Place	P. MacRannall	8	15.00	5.00
The Chip II	S. Wilson	4	15.00	5.00

Query your tables to display the following information:

a. Boat name, captain, and gallons per hour with a tonnage equal to 8.
b. Boat name, length, and deck hands carrying for boats 50 or fewer passengers.
c. Boat name, gallons per hour, deck hands, with a license of LOC (refer to exercise 3 for further license definitions).
d. Captain name and boat name where the number of passengers is greater than 150.
e. Boat name, captain name, captain's wage where the tonnage is greater than 25 and the speed is greater than 8 knots.
f. Use an ALIAS to locate boat name, license, length of boat/feet, and number of deck hands for all boats carrying 50 or more passengers.
g. Use the IN operator to display all columns in the **charter** table where the **crew** table shows a wage greater than 15.00.
h. Use the EXISTS operator to locate all boats with a license of I. Display the boat name and license only.

ANSWERS TO THE RECALL QUESTIONS

1. Joining tables recognizes relationships that exist between two or more tables. Queries may be performed on tables separately, but the joining of tables allows queries to be performed that will draw information out of multiple tables in a single command.

2. SELECT authors.name, publishers.name, publishers.city FROM authors, publishers WHERE authors.city = publishers.city

3. SELECT authors.aname, publishers.pname, critics.cname, authors.city FROM authors, publishers, critics WHERE authors.city = publishers.city AND authors.authid = publishers.pubid

4. An ALIAS is a second name given to a table when the table is copied to itself. It is used to compare values of rows containing common field values.

5. A subquery allows for an inner query to be performed within an outer query. Generally the inner query is searching for a "true" condition that is then used by the outer query.

6. In a correlated subquery, each row is evaluated separately. Different answers may be generated for each row of a table addressed in the outer query.

7. The ANY operator must select values in the subquery of the same type as found in the outer query.

8. With the ALL operator, every value of the subquery must satisfy the condition of the outer query.

PART 4
VIEWS OF DATA

CHAPTER 8
CREATING VIEWS

PREVIEW

A view is a collection of various values from more than one table. The contents of a view are taken from a query command. Throughout the exercises you have completed thus far, you have been working with "base tables." Base tables contain data values. Views are another kind of table. Their values are taken from the base tables. A view table does not, however, contain any of its own data. Again, it contains combinations of data values from other tables. It is a way of looking at the data in our base tables differently. When you give a view command, you create output that is a part of the columns and table names you have used in the command.

CREATING VIEWS

Suppose you wanted to create a view of the all customers living in Washington State from the **customers** table. A simple view command creates a new view that contains this information.

1. Type:

```
CREATE VIEW wacustomers AS SELECT * FROM customers
    WHERE state = 'WA'
```

This command created the new view table called **wacustomers**. You can now use this view as you would any other table. You can add row to it, query it, update the rows, insert and delete from the view table, and use JOIN commands with the view.

2. Type:

```
SELECT * FROM wacustomers
```

This command enables you to view all of your columns and the data values therein. As you can see, this view contains all customers from the State of Washington, as shown in Figure 4.1.

custid	fname	address	city
11	Frances Gates	300 Brighton St.	Seattle
12	Lloyd Ohlsen	103 First Avenue	Seattle
13	Yvonne Lewis	1515 N.E. 50th	Kirkland
14	Dale Glenn	2518 25th N.E.	Redmond
15	Robert Hill	15 Union Rd.	Spokane

Figure 4.1 Results of a View

The primary advantage in creating a view like this one is that when you update the base table, **customers**, or any other base table with information that will affect a view table, the view table will automatically be updated; therefore, without performing lengthy queries, you can always look at the view to check on the current status of a particular column or columns. In this case, you can add to the **customers** table and at any time look at the view table to see how many additional customers there are in Washington State.

To Create Views of Specific Columns

You can create views that contain only specific columns for data values as well.

1. Type:

```
CREATE VIEW hired AS SELECT repid, repfname, hiredate
    FROM salesreps
```

This command creates the view of the **repid**, **repfname**, and **hiredate** of sales representatives from the **salesreps** table shown in Figure 4.2.

2. Type:

```
SELECT * FROM hired
```

to see the results shown in Figure 4.2.

repid	repfname	hiredate
1	Alex Baldwin	11/05/87
2	Judy Marshall	05/04/89
3	Karen Anderson	07/16/88
4	Roger Maltby	03/10/86
5	Morris Crenshaw	10/21/89

Figure 4.2 Results of a view on specific columns

To Update a View

You can update a view just as you would a base table. Any updates are automatically performed on the view as well as the base table. While there are some restrictions on updates (discussed later in this chapter), the following example shows you how a simple update works with views.

1. Type:

   UPDATE wacustomers SET fname = 'Lloyd Olsen' WHERE fname = 'Lloyd Ohlsen'

This command will update the view and the **customers** table, as shown in Figure 4.3.

2. Type:

   SELECT * FROM customers

to view the change.

custid	fname	address	city
11	Frances Gates	300 Brighton St.	Seattle
12	Lloyd Olsen	103 First Avenue	Seattle
13	Yvonne Lewis	1515 N.E. 50th	Kirkland
14	Dale Glenn	2518 25th N.E.	Redmond
15	Robert Hill	15 Union Rd.	Spokane

Figure 4.3 Results of updating a view

To Query a View

You can see the value of views when you begin to query a view rather than the base table, as in the following example:

Type:

```
SELECT * FROM wacustomers WHERE city = 'Seattle'
```

The results are those of Figure 4.4.

custid	fname	address	city
11	Frances Gates	300 Brighton St.	Seattle
12	Lloyd Olsen	103 First Avenue	Seattle

Figure 4.4 Results of querying a view

As the views may become more complex, you can see the advantage of having a part of the query already performed and waiting in a view.

To Group Views with COUNT and SUM

Grouped views are used to avoid the necessity of repeating complex queries. Suppose you have a very lengthy **sales** table and that you need to keep track of all sales made by the individual representatives on a daily basis as well as the total net amount, the total tax, and the gross total. This could be a lengthy process if you had to type a query of the **sales** table each time. Instead, you can do the following:

1. Type:

```
CREATE VIEW dailytot AS SELECT invdate, COUNT
    (DISTINCT repid), SUM (DISTINCT netamt), SUM
    (DISTINCT tax), SUM (DISTINCT totamt) FROM sales
    GROUP BY invdate
```

2. Look at the new view:

```
SELECT * FROM dailytot
```

In step 1, you created a view called **dailytot**. You selected the columns **repid**, **netamt**, **tax**, and **totamt** as columns that were going to be counted or whose sums were going to be computed. The columns were from the **sales** table and were grouped by **invdate**. Remember that as you update the sales table, the view is also updated and so you never need to write the query command again. Step 2 is the only step that needs to be performed from now on to see the daily totals. The results of this query are shown in Figure 4.5.

invdate	count (dis	sum (distinct n	sum (distinct t	sum (distinct t
01/07/90	1	$350.00	$21.00	$371.00
01/28/90	1	$225.00	$13.50	$238.00
02/15/90	1	$90.00	$7.29	$97.29
02/23/90	1	$150.00	$12.15	$162.15
02/26/90	1	$75.00	$6.08	$81.08
03/01/90	1	$175.00	$14.00	$189.00

Figure 4.5 Results of a view using COUNT and SUM

To Use a View with Join Operation

You can also join two or more tables in a view. You can look at the invoice date, the representative name, and the total amount of a sale from both the **salesreps** table and the **sales** table.

1. Type:

   CREATE VIEW invday AS SELECT invdate, totamt,
   a.repfname FROM salesreps a, sales b WHERE a.repid =
   b.repid

2. View the results of the command by typing:

   SELECT * FROM invday WHERE repfname = 'Judy Marshall'

will produce a table showing only the Judy Marshall row with the invoice date and total amount of the sale.

To Drop a View

You can drop a view in much the same way that you drop a base table. Do not drop a view at this time, but look at the syntax for doing so shown below.

DROP VIEW <view name>

UPDATING VIEWS

When you update views, remember that you are also updating the tables referenced in the view. As you have learned, a view consists of the results of a query. The results are something saved in a table that does not contain its own data, but rather the data of a table or multiple tables.

There are some restrictions to updating views that need to be mentioned and remembered by the user. They are

* The view must be from a query performed on only one table.
* The view must include the primary key of the one table.
* The view cannot use DISTINCT, GROUP BY, or HAVING in its definition.
* The view cannot include subqueries.
* The view cannot contain constants, strings, or value expressions such as 250 * .10.
* When using the INSERT update command, the view must not contain any NOT NULL columns.

Note: The DISTINCT and GROUP BY were used on the previous page in the COUNT and SUM commands. This use is different from actually updating the view, as shown in the following steps.

You may be wondering why all the restrictions on updating views. It is simple. Views draw information from a table or tables; however, they do not make comparisons of rows or derive information about them. As mentioned, you cannot use joins and subqueries with DISTINCT, which compares table rows in a complex manner. Because of the more specialized and sophisticated querying techniques used in queries from base tables, views cannot be compared to the standard query operations. Because the base tables contain data values and the views do not, you must have a rather simple view to perform updates that will easily be transferred to the base table. When the views become too complex, you are no longer allowed to affect the base tables. Updates of a complex nature in a view command would be too complex for the system to handle. When a view table has update restrictions on it, it is considered to be a *read-only* view. Read-only views are any views that do not follow the criteria listed above.

Read-only views do, however, allow you the advantage of having on hand very complex views of data that you can access without writing lengthy queries every time. You can now see the advantages of both updatable views and read-only views.

To Write an Updatable View

The following is an example of an updatable view.

1. Type:

```
CREATE VIEW cityca AS SELECT * FROM customers
    WHERE state = 'CA'
```

This command follows all of the restrictions needed in a view in order for it to be updated and produces the results of the two cities located in California as shown in Figure 4.6.

custid	fname	address	city
19	Jean Randolph	101 Mariposa	Fresno
20	Tom Cranston	15 Seneca St.	Oakland

Figure 4.6 Results of writing an updatable view

2. Type:

```
CREATE VIEW custname AS SELECT fname, address, city,
    state FROM customers WHERE custid <> 1
```

This is also an updatable command. It draws data from a single table, as did the first command; it uses multiple columns, which is not one of the restrictions; and it looks for all values of custid were the value is not equal to 1, as shown in Figure 4.7. Both of the commands are within the guidelines of the restrictions listed earlier.

fname	address	city	state
------------------	---------------------	-----------	---------
Frances Gates	300 Brighton St.	Seattle	WA
Lloyd Olsen	103 First Avenue	Seattle	WA
Yvonne Lewis	1515 N.E. 50th	Kirkland	WA
Dale Glenn	2518 25th N.E.	Redmond	WA
Robert Hill	15 Union Rd.	Spokane	WA
Rachel Cole	1600 Creekside Dr.	Portland	OR
Susan Leland	5157 Caribou Ave.	Anchorage	AK
Donn Hansen	900 Deep Freeze Ct.	Fairbanks	AK
Jean Randolph	101 Mariposa	Fresno	CA
Tom Cranston	15 Seneca St.	Oakland	CA

Figure 4.7 Results of a second updatable command

To Check the Values in a View

One of the tricky aspects of updating views is that you must be certain what the original view did. If, for example, you created a view from the **sales** table called **salestotal** that contained all **totamt** values greater than 200.00, then performed an update on the **salestotal** view to add values less than 200.00 to a row, the update would not work.

There is a way that you can check the values of a view. It is done using the WITH CHECK OPTION. This option is included in the original definition of the view. To write a view that draws information from the **sales** table, as stated in the previous paragraph and that includes the WITH CHECK OPTION,

Type:

```
CREATE VIEW salestotal AS SELECT invid, invdate, totamt
    FROM sales WHERE totamt > 200.00 WITH CHECK
    OPTION
```

When this option statement is included in the command, no illegal updates are allowed. If you try to update the view with a value less than 200.00, you receive a message rejecting your attempt. If you plan to update single-table views very often, you may want to include this option every time you create a new updatable view.

It might also be wise to include in your view all columns in the table. In that way, your updates are not rejected when you try to include a column not selected in the original view. Looking at the example above, you used only the **invid**, **invdate**, and **totamt** columns. Trying to update any other columns will result in a rejection message. For that reason, you may want to write the AS SELECT line as:

```
AS SELECT *
```

which would include all columns.

To Insert New Values

Work with the view **salestotal** just created. It contains the columns **invid**, **invdate**, and **totamt** from the **sales** table for all values greater than 200.00.

1. Type:

```
INSERT into sales VALUES
    (117,3/10/90,2,12,224.32,54.00,278.32)
```

This will add a new row to the view **salestotal**.

2. Type:

```
SELECT * FROM salestotal
```

The results are shown in Figure 4.8.

invid	invdate	totamt
111	01/07/90	$371.00
112	01/28/90	$238.00
117	03/10/90	$278.32

Figure 4.8 Results of inserting new values in the **sales** table

You could update the customers table through the view custname to change the address of one of the customers.

3. Type:

```
UPDATE custname SET address = '2130 Kodiak Bear Lane'
    WHERE fname = 'Susan Leland'
```

This will update customer 17, Susan Leland, to include her new address.

4. View the custname view to see the change.

You could also use the DELETE command. An example follows for your reference; however, do not delete at this time.

```
DELETE from custname WHERE fname = 'Robert Hill'
```

5. Type:

SELECT * FROM **custname**

to view the table shown in Figure 4.9.

custid	fname	address	city
11	Frances Gates	300 Brighton St.	Seattle
12	Lloyd Olsen	103 First Avenue	Seattle
13	Yvonne Lewis	1515 N.E. 50th	Kirkland
14	Dale Glenn	2518 25th N.E.	Redmond
16	Rachel Cole	1600 Creekside Dr.	Portland
17	Susan Leland	2130 Kodiak Bear Lane	Anchorage
18	Donn Hansen	900 Deep Freeze Ct.	Fairbanks
19	Jean Randolph	101 Mariposa	Fresno
20	Tom Cranston	15 Seneca St.	Oakland

Figure 4.9 Result of using the DELETE command

Summary

Once you have mastered the simple guidelines of writing updatable views, you can then apply more update commands using INSERT, UPDATE, and DELETE. Be especially careful with the DELETE command: You may remember from Chapter 3 that the command *DELETE from customers;* would remove all rows from a table. This command was used prior to removing the table itself.

REINFORCEMENT EXERCISES

RECALL QUESTIONS

1. Write a simple command to create a view on the table called **inventory** that will display a view of the **totinv** at any given time and will select all columns from the table for values less than 100. Call the view **currentinv**.

2. What command would you use to display the results of the above view?

3. Write an AS SELECT command that will display selected columns of a table. Use your own column names for the example.

4. Write an UPDATE command for changing the address and city of a customer. Use your own column names for the example.

5. What is the main advantage of grouping views?

6. How are table names identified when joining more than one table in a view? Write an example of a FROM command that shows the table names being queried.

7. What commands or clauses may not be included when updating a view?

8. How many tables may a view consist of in order to be updated?

9. What is the purpose of checking the values in a view?

10. Give an example of inserting new values into a view. Use your own view name and values.

PRACTICE EXERCISE 5

For this exercise, use the tables created in Parts 2 and 3: charters, crew, and gallons.

1. Create a view called **license** that shows all columns of the **charters** table where the **license** is equal to **LOC**. Include a CHECK WITH OPTION.

2. View the new table created in step 1 called **license**.

3. Create a view called **captain**. Use only columns **captain, license,** and **tonnage** from the charters table and then look at the new view table.

4. Update the view called **captain** to include a change of captain's name. The update will be on the captain of the **Easy Days**. The new captain is A. Strouss.

5. Query the **license** view to show all boats with a license equal to LIC and a length of 50 or more feet.

6. Create a view called **deckhands** that will count the total **deck hands** and **sum** all deck hands wages of all boats from the **crew** table. Group by **boat name**.

7. Join the tables **crew** and **gallons**. Create a view called **wages** that will display the length of the boat, the boat name, and the number of deck hands per boat.

8. Drop the view called **wages** created in step 7.

9. Update the **license** view to change the license type of registration number WN2911L to LIC. What happened?

10. Insert the new values into the **deckhands** view. The new values are:

    a. Deck hands have increased to 3 on the Spirit of Eagle Harbor.
    b. The deck hand wages have been increased for all boats to 5.50 an hour.

ANSWERS TO THE RECALL QUESTIONS

1. CREATE VIEW currentinv AS SELECT * FROM inventory WHERE totinv < 100

2. SELECT * FROM currentinv

3. AS SELECT col1, col2, col3

4. UPDATE viewname SET address = '1879 N.E. 23rd' SET city = 'Anchorage' WHERE fname = 'Jane Doe'

5. It avoids having to repeat complex queries. It is best used when keeping track of information from tables on a daily basis.

6. FROM sales a, sales b

7. DISTINCT, GROUP BY, and HAVING

8. one

9. The CHECK OPTION command can be used to assure that no illegal values are entered into a view when updating.

10. INSERT into charters VALUES (R. Sanderson) WHERE captain = 'J. Paton'

NOTES

PART 5
PRIVILEGES AND GLOBAL FUNCTIONS

CHAPTER 9
DETERMINING USER PRIVILEGES

PREVIEW

SQL is often used in environments that require a differentiation between numerous users of the system. Privileges determine whether or not a user can perform certain commands on tables. Quite often in a large mainframe environment there is a database administrator who oversees who the users are and who can sign onto the system, but users themselves have some control over who can do what to their tables.

Users who are required to have an identifying number when entering the SQL environment are recognized by SQL as that number. It is through the identification number that users are granted or revoked privileges. The identifying number may be used as the logon process in a multiuser environment. In most circumstances each user will have his or her own logon number or user ID. In some circumstances, however, a user may have access to more than one user ID or a single ID may be used by multiple users. In these instances, SQL again refers only to the user ID and assumes that the ID being used (regardless of the number of users) has authorization.

In this chapter, you will learn how to apply privilcgc commands when working in a networked or mainframe environment. The instructions will be presented so that anyone working in this type of environment may experiment with them. Microcomputer users will be able to implement these instructions.

USER PRIVILEGES

Privileges can be given to particular users on particular tables or views. These privileges are commonly referred to as *object privileges.* Any user who creates a table has the ownership of that table and can decide all privileges associated with the table. Those that the user can assign are listed in Table 6.1.

SELECT	The ability of the user to perform queries on a table.
INSERT	The ability of the user to apply the insert command on a table.
UPDATE	The ability of the user to perform update procedures on a table.
DELETE	The ability of the user to perform delete operations on a table.
REFERENCES	The ability of the user to define foreign keys that use one or more columns of a table as a parent key.

Table 6.1 List of Object Privileges

Any assignment of privileges given to a user are done through the GRANT command.

USING THE GRANT COMMAND

Assume that you are working in a network environment and that your password is your first name. If you want to grant privileges on **customers** table to another using his or her password, the command would be:

```
GRANT SELECT ON customers TO sharon
```

With this command, Sharon can perform queries on a table you have created. With this simple grant, Sharon can only perform SELECT commands on the tables and will not be allowed to insert or otherwise modify the table. It can only be queried.

To Grant Additional Privileges

If you want someone to be allowed to insert new values into a table, you write:

```
GRANT INSERT ON customers TO peter
```

Peter now has the privilege of inserting new customers into your table.

If you decide to allow Sharon and Peter to be able to add data values and to query one of your tables, you write:

GRANT SELECT, INSERT ON salesreps TO sharon, peter

Using this example, you can grant many commands to many different users.

Sharon can also be allowed to update a table with the following command:

GRANT UPDATE ON salesreps TO sharon

To Restrict Privileges

Suppose, however, that you want to restrict Peter's use of the update privileges on the **salesreps** table. You can write the following command:

GRANT UPDATE (commiss) ON salesreps TO peter

This command restricts Peter's updating to only the **commiss** column in the **salesreps** table.

You can also grant privileges on multiple columns in a table.

GRANT UPDATE (repid, repfname) ON salesreps TO sharon

In this instance, Sharon has privileges that include the ability to update the **salesreps** table only through the **repid** and **repfname** columns.

To Grant References

Granting references to a user allows that person to use tables as parent keys. *Parent keys* are tables whose columns are referenced by a column in another table. A parent column may be **repid** used in the **salesreps** table. When that same column is used again in the **sales** table, it is said to be referencing the *parent column.* The secondary column in the **sales** table is referred to as the *foreign key.* Privileges can also be given to specific columns within the table that may be used as parent keys, as in the following command.

GRANT REFERENCES (custid, fname, state) ON customers
TO sharon

Privileges may also be given to allow access to all columns of a table for use as parent keys, using the command below:

GRANT REFERENCES ON sales TO peter

To Grant ALL and PUBLIC Privileges

You can grant special privileges to users that encompass a greater span than those previously introduced. One is the ALL privilege, which grants all rights to the designated user. The other is PUBLIC, which grants privileges to all users.

To grant privileges to Peter, for example, that would include all rights on a table, you would type:

```
GRANT ALL PRIVILEGES ON sales TO peter
```

To grant all privileges to any user, you would type:

```
GRANT SELECT ON sales TO PUBLIC
```

Granting privileges to the public should be done with caution. This command grants privileges to every user, regardless of how long he or she has had access to SQL. With this command, the user has all rights to modify, query, delete, insert, etc., any one of your tables.

To Grant Privileges with a Grant Option

At times it might be useful for the user not only to grant privileges to another user but also to allow that user to grant options to other users as well. This is particularly useful when another person might be taking over the handling of tables for an extended period of time. It is also useful in large corporations where the person creating the database then delegates responsibility of adding values, modifying, and other functions to others.

If Sharon decided to give Peter the right to grant the SELECT privilege on the **salesreps** table, for example, she would give him the WITH GRANT OPTION as shown below:

```
GRANT SELECT ON salesreps TO peter WITH GRANT
    OPTION
```

Peter would then have the right to give privileges to a third party with a command such as:

```
GRANT SELECT ON sharon.salesreps TO selena
```

He could also grant the third person the right of grant option with a command such as:

```
GRANT SELECT ON sharon.salesreps TO selena WITH
    GRANT OPTION
```

As you can see, giving Peter the grant option allows Peter a great deal of privilege with respect to this table and allows Peter the right to delegate the access to a table to others. The table's owner, however, is always known through the name preceding the table name. This command simply allows for a great deal of flexibility and access to tables when needed.

REMOVING PRIVILEGES

Through the use of the REVOKE command, you can remove the privileges assigned to users. The syntax is similar to the GRANT with the word REVOKE substituted.

To remove the privileges granted originally to Sharon on the customers table, you would type:

```
REVOKE INSERT ON Orders FROM sharon
```

You can also specify privileges and users such as in the following command revoking privileges given to Sharon and Peter.

```
REVOKE INSERT , DELETE ON salesreps FROM sharon,
    peter
```

USING VIEWS FOR PRIVILEGES

Another option in assigning privileges to users is to create views directed to the specific user. In order to create the view, you must have full privileges yourself to the table with all rights. Generally speaking, you will create views that grant privileges on your own tables or on any tables to which you have been granted full privilege.

If you want to give Selena the ability to see only the **repid**, **netamt**, **tax**, and **totamt** from the **sales** table, you could write:

```
CREATE VIEW selenaview AS SELECT netamt, tax, and
    totamt FROM sales
```

This command would grant Selena privileges on the view and the information contained in the view (those columns listed) but not on the **sales** table itself.

There are other ways to grant privileges in views as well. You can limit the privilege to particular rows. To do this, you would create a view as you would normally and then assign that view to the grantee. An example of this might be:

```
CREATE VIEW custview AS SELECT * FROM customers
    WHERE city = ‘Seattle’ WITH CHECK OPTION
```

The WITH CHECK OPTION prevents the grantee from changing the **city** column to any value other than Seattle.

If you then wanted to grant privileges on this view to Selena, you would type:

```
GRANT UPDATE ON custview TO Selena
```

GRANTING SYSTEM PRIVILEGES

At this highest level, one of the concerns in working with any database management system is who has the right to create databases, tables, and views and to access and update or modify them regularly. You can imagine a situation in which any user of a large corporation had the right to sign onto the system and design database tables and views. The chaos this would probably create could be enormous and cause unimaginable data redundancy. Therefore, there must be some control over who creates and designs the primary database tables, who is allowed to modify them, and who is allowed to access them for queries and designing views.

SQL commands include some system privileges to handle these problems. Three of the most common system privileges are:

CONNECT
RESOURCE
DBA

CONNECT allows the right to log on and create views when granted the correct privileges. RESOURCE allows the user the right to create base tables. DBA (Database Administrator) is the highest privilege and allows the user the right of total or carte-blanche authority over the entire database system. Any one of these privileges will be acknowledged by the system through the user ID. To give some order to the control of privileges to users, the DBA may be the one to assign specific privileges through the GRANT RESOURCE command. This command would allow a user to create a table and is written as:

```
GRANT RESOURCE TO steve
```

To Add or Delete Users

Other tasks generally handled by the DBA are those of assigning new users and passwords and of deleting users. An example of assigning a new user with his or her password is shown below:

```
GRANT CONNECT TO patrick IDENTIFIED BY delano
```

This command assigns the new user Patrick the status of connect and assigns him the password "delano" at the same time. If the user is deleted later or access is denied, then the REVOKE command must be used and the user is deleted from the system. In this instance, the command REVOKE simply replaces the GRANT command.

CHAPTER 10
GLOBAL FEATURES OF SQL

PREVIEW

SQL has aspects of its commands that are relevant to the database as a whole. Many of these tasks are handled by database administrators (DBA's) and will not be reviewed in detail here. Some of the global commands with which you may have encounters in the future, however, are those concerned with creating synonyms (aliases) for table names. This is a particularly useful feature that allows the user to shorten or personalize the name of a table on which privileges have been granted.

CREATING DIFFERENT TABLE NAMES

You learned in Chapter 9 that you can access another person's table by referring to the table and the owner's name. Once you have been given privileges to that table, you can use it in commands in this manner. It can, however, be time consuming and lengthy to always have to remember the owner's name or to simply have to type it out every time you are referring to a particular table in a command. For this reason, SQL allows you to create synonyms for tables. A synonym is an alternative name for a table. When you create the synonym, you own the table and no longer need to precede the table name with the owner's name. You need only refer to it by its alternative name.

To create a synonym, you need only have one or more privileges on the table. The privileges you have will not change, however. You will still be limited and the same privileges will exist as they were granted by the owner.

To Create a New Name

Suppose you wanted to create a synonym for the **salesreps** table on which privileges have been granted to you from owner Melissa. You could create a new and shorter version of the original table name that will be yours to use in each command. You would write:

```
CREATE SYNONYM reps FOR selena.salesreps
```

Now you would be able to use the table name **reps** for every occurrence of the table granted you, called **selena.salesreps.**

To Create the Same Name

Another option is to use the same table name as the original, thus creating a synonym with the same name. This makes it easier to remember the table to which the synonym is referencing, but may not necessarily be all that much shorter than with the owner's name attached. The decision would be up to you in any given situation. Such a command would be written the same as when creating a new name for the table:

CREATE SYNONYM salesreps FOR selena.salesreps

SQL now recognizes two different tables: the **selena.salesreps** table and your table, recognized as **yourname.salesreps**.

To Create a Name for All Users

You can use a command similar to the two previous ones by creating a name for the public (all users). If you were the owner of the salesreps table, this command would read:

CREATE PUBLIC SYNONYM salesreps FOR salesreps

Had you not been the owner, the last salesreps would need to be preceded by the owner's name. Otherwise, it is assumed that you are creating this synonym for all users with privileges on the **salesreps** table. This kind of public synonym is usually granted by the database administrator (DBA). The privilege to drop public synonyms would also belong to the DBA.

To Drop a Synonym

A synonym is dropped by its owner (with the exception of the public synonyms as stated above).

For you to drop the synonym called **reps** on the **salesreps** table, you would type:

DROP SYNONYM reps

NOTES

PART 6
EMBEDDED SQL

CHAPTER 11
USING SQL IN PROGRAMS

PREVIEW

It is possible to embed SQL commands in programming languages such as COBOL and other high-level computer languages. Those supporting SQL are Pascal, FORTRAN, PL/I, and C. The method with which SQL can be embedded in a program is similar from program to program. If you are familiar with a high-level language, you will see from the examples that other modules could be written using another language that would perform the same function. In this chapter, you will see several examples of embedded SQL commands within various programs. These examples are for your reference and may be applied as you have the necessity or desire to do so.

EMBEDDING SQL

SQL commands are located in the source code of the host program. The SQL commands always begin with the phrase EXEC SQL and end with END-EXEC. It is important to note that when compiling embedded SQL modules in a program, it is a requirement that the program be precompiled before it is compiled. A program called a precompiler (sometimes referred to as preprocessor) will convert SQL commands to a form usable by the host language. The compiler is then used to convert the program to source code.

Several examples of embedded SQL commands are listed below. They are followed by some specific COBOL examples. The examples below are shown as they could be inserted into any of the high-level host languages listed above with possibly some variations, depending upon the restrictions of the particular language (such things as whether or not to end the command with the END-EXEC command used in COBOL or with a semicolon [;] at the end of the command).

To Insert Values into a Table

Column names are distinguished and identified with the host column names through the use of a colon (:) in front of each column name. To insert a set of values from your program into the **customers** table, for example, you would:

Type:

```
EXEC SQL INSERT INTO customers VALUES (:custid,
    :fname, :address, :city, :state)
```

When using Pascal or PL/I, a semicolon is inserted at the end of the command. As you will see in the following COBOL examples, the END-EXEC command is used in COBOL instructions. No end mark is required when using FORTRAN.

To Declare Variables

You can declare variables through the use of a DECLARE SECTION using the host language syntax. You may include any number of sections in a program, such as in the following example, showing a Pascal module.

```
EXEC SQL BEGIN DECLARE SECTION;
Var
    custid:     integer;
    fname:      packed array (1..10) of char;
    address:    packed array (1..10) of char;
    city:       packed array (1..10) of char;
    state:      packed array (1..10) of char;
EXEC SQL END DECLARE SECTION;
```

This module begins with a list of the variables to be inserted. The variables are introduced with the *Var* heading. The packed arrays hold a series of values. The use of the semicolon (;) at the end of each definition is required of Pascal commands but is not necessary when using SQL.

To Retrieve Values INTO Variables

You can also insert values from a SQL table into the host language variables using the INTO command. An example of this type of command follows:

```
EXEC SQL SELECT custid, fname, address, city, state INTO
    :custid, :fname, :address, :city, :state FROM customers
    WHERE custid = 17;
```

You can see the similarity to a regular SQL command in the use of SELECT, INTO, FROM, and WHERE commands. The difference lies again in the use of the colon (:) preceding the variable, names of the host language.

USING THE CURSOR

This type of cursor does not refer to the blinking cursor that marks your position on the screen; it does, however, refer to a device that marks your place in the output of a query. The advantage of this function is that you can assign the output of a query to variables even though you do not know how much output will result.

Another way to look at the cursor is as a type of variable that is associated with a query. The value of the variable will be each row of the query's output. The DECLARE CURSOR command declares the introduction of the cursor variable, similar to declaring variables in the DECLARE module. An example of the cursor declaration is:

```
EXEC SQL DECLARE CURSOR allcust FOR SELECT *
    FROM customers WHERE custid >10;
```

After this command is written, it is not immediately executed. It takes an OPEN command to actually start the count of the content of the cursor.

```
EXEC SQL OPEN CURSOR allcust;
```

Next, the FETCH command is used to actually extract the output from the query. The output appears one row at a time (for each FETCH command), ordered as it had located the rows.

```
EXEC SQL FETCH allcust INTO :custid, :fname, :address,
:city, :state;
```

This final command in the sequence inserts the values into the variables in the host program. Because each FETCH command will extract only one row and another FETCH command would be needed to extract a second row, it is best to place the FETCH within a loop. When looking at the loop instructions, you can see the advantage of the cursor function. It allows you to decide when you want to stop viewing the rows located. This is helpful when perhaps hundreds or thousands of rows contain the results of a query.

```
Advance_a_row: = True;
    EXEC SQL OPEN CURSOR allcust;
        while Advance_a_row do
            begin
            EXEC SQL FETCH allcust
            INTO :custid, :fname, :address, :city, :state;
            writeln (custid, fname, address, city, state);
            writeln ('Do you want to see the next row? (Y/N)');
            readln (response);
            if response = 'N' then Advance_a_row: = False
            end;
        EXEC SQL CLOSE CURSOR allcust;
```

While this is a Pascal example, you may be able to see the similarities and changes that would occur in other high-level languages such as C, COBOL, and PL/I. In this example, the Boolean variable called Advance_a_row is set to True. The cursor *allcust* is opened and the loop begins with the *while* instruction. Within the loop, the SQL command is executed and the *allcust* cursor is fetched. Data is read one row at a time into the host program variables that begin with a colon. The first row is output to the screen in the writeln command. A question appears asking the user whether or not he or she wants to view the next row. The response is noted. An 'N' response will result in a *false* condition and the loop will end; otherwise a *true* condition will exist and the loop will repeat.

USING SQL WITH COBOL

In a COBOL program, SQL commands are included in both the DATA and PROCEDURE divisions in addition to the regular COBOL instructions. They are defined as follows:

In the DATA DIVISION:

> Tables are declared that will be used in processing the data.

In the PROCEDURE DIVISION:

> SQL commands are used to retrieve rows, insert rows, update existing rows, delete rows, and so on.

The beginning and ending statements used within the program are

```
EXEC SQL
```

and

```
END-EXEC
```

This alerts the compiler to the beginning and end of the SQL statements.

The DATA DIVISON

As mentioned above, any tables that are going to be declared in a COBOL program must be done in the DATA DIVISON. Within the DATA DIVISION, tables are processed in the WORKING-STORAGE instructions. The processing is accomplished with the DECLARE TABLE command, which is similar to the CREATE TABLE command in SQL.

The **customers** table was used throughout this text as an example. It is shown here for reference.

```
CREATE TABLE customers
    (custid     integer NOT NULL PRIMARY KEY,
    name        char(20) NOT NULL,
    address     char(25),
    city        char(15),
    state       char(2);
```

To process this table in a COBOL program, you would write:

```
EXEC SQL
    DECLARE CUSTOMERS TABLE
        (CUSTID      INTEGER (2),
         NAME        CHAR (20),
         ADDRESS     CHAR (25),
         CITY        CHAR (15),
         STATE       CHAR (2))
END-EXEC.
```

If this table had been stored previously in a library, you would then write:

```
EXEC SQL
    INCLUDE CUSTOMERS
END-EXEC.
```

When processing the table, you will need to use the regular COBOL variables for each of the columns in the table. For the instructions shown above where the table was processed, your definitions would be similar to the ones shown below. This time you do not need to precede the instructions with EXEC SQL and END-EXEC because these lines return to standard COBOL instructions.

```
01 W-CUSTOMERS
        03 CUSTID                PIC S9(2)      COMP-3.
        03 NAME                  PIC X(20).
        03 ADDRESS               PIC X(25).
        03 CITY                  PIC X(15).
        03 STATE                 PIC X(2).
```

The PROCEDURE DIVISION

If normal COBOL variables are used in SQL commands within a program, they must be preceded by a colon (:). In the examples above, for instance, the variables are listed using the standard COBOL format (called *host variables*). If you use the same variables in a SQL command within the program, precede them with the colon, for example, :CUSTID.

The results of any SQL queries must also be placed in a host variable, using the INTO clause. The following command shows an example of this:

```
SELECT name
    INTO :NAME
    FROM customers
    WHERE STATE = 'WA';
```

To Retrieve a Row

To retrieve a row within a COBOL program, you can see the similarities to retrieving with SQL alone.

Using SQL Alone:

```
SELECT name
    FROM customers
    WHERE state = 'OR';
```

Using COBOL:

```
EXEC SQL
    SELECT NAME
        INTO :NAME
        FROM CUSTOMERS
        WHERE STATE = 'WA'
END-EXEC.
```

To Retrieve All Columns

You can retrieve all columns from a table in much the same way you retrieve a single row. When you do so, all columns are selected using the SQL column names and moved into the COBOL variable names (introduced with a colon), as in the following example:

```
EXEC SQL
    SELECT CUSTID, NAME, ADDRESS, CITY, STATE
        INTO :CUSTID, :NAME, :ADDRESS, :CITY, :STATE
    FROM CUSTOMERS
    WHERE CUSTID = :CUSTID
END-EXEC.
```

To Insert a Row

You can add a row to the **customers** table within a COBOL program as well. The INSERT command is used to add a row, as follows:

```
EXEC SQL
    INSERT
        INTO CUSTOMERS
        VALUES (:CUSTID, :NAME, :ADDRESS, :CITY,
    :STATE)
END-EXEC.
```

The values are contained in the host variables, so they are preceded by colons.

To Change the Value of a Row:

You can change the value of a row in a table just as you would in the straight SQL commands. The UPDATE command is used to accomplish the change. Look at the following COBOL example. You can see the similarity to SQL instructions used alone.

```
EXEC SQL
    UPDATE CUSTOMERS
        SET NAME = :NAME
        WHERE CITY = :CITY
END-EXEC.
```

The name of the customer whose city is currently stored in CITY will change to the value currently stored in NAME.

SUMMARY

When integrating SQL commands into COBOL instructions, you should remember some common rules:

* Use SELECT statements as embedded SQL commands to retrieve only a single row.
* Use the INTO clause in a SELECT command to place the results of a SELECT statement into host language variables.
* Use INSERT, UPDATE, and DELETE statements to affect one or more rows.

There is much you can do with cursors. This text introduces cursors as a feature that plays an important role in retrieving rows through a SQL command. A cursor acts like a pointer to a row in a group of rows being retrieved. The cursor can be advanced one row at a time to produce sequential, one-record-at-a-time row retrieval. You may want to locate an extensive COBOL text that includes detailed information on cursors as used with COBOL or check your programming text for information on this feature in the language you are using.

APPENDIX I
QUICK REFERENCE GUIDE

PREVIEW

The Quick Reference Guide provides an alphabetical list that summarizes the various procedures learned in this text. After completing the lessons, use the guide to assist you with SQL functions as you need them. Examples are shown as they were presented in the text, using table names (**customers**, **sales**, and **salesreps**) and column names (as shown in Chapter 1) for which other names can be substituted as appropriate.

ADDING A NEW COLUMN

This command adds a new column to an existing table.

Example:

ALTER TABLE sales ADD totamt CURRENCY

In this example, the new column **totamt** is added to the **sales** table. The type is also assigned as currency.

ADDING DATA VALUES TO A TABLE

Once a table is created, this command inserts data values into the table a row at a time in exactly the order in which the columns were originally created in the base table.

Example:

INSERT INTO customers VALUES (11, 'Frances Gates','300 Brighton St.','Seattle','WA')

The above INSERT command has added the values within the parentheses into the table called **customers**. Every TEXT column must be inserted in quotes, all integer columns do not require quotes.

ALIAS

An alias is used to give a new name to an existing table. The alias then is used throughout the remainder of the command. When an alias is assigned in a command, it is immediately preceded by the base table name.

Example:

```
SELECT first.city, second.city, first.fname FROM customers
    first, salesreps second WHERE first.city = second.city
```

In this example, **customers** is given the alias of *first* and **salesreps** is given the alias of *second*. Notice then, that the alias names, *first* and *second* are used in the WHERE clause.

ALL OPERATOR

The ALL operator is used when every value of the subquery must satisfy the condition of the outer query.

Example:

```
SELECT * FROM salesreps WHERE commiss > ALL
    (SELECT commiss FROM salesreps WHERE city =
    'Portland')
```

This particular command searches for a condition in the inner loop that is equal to Portland. When that condition is found, the outer loop searches for all conditions in the table that are greater than those in the inner loop.

ANY OR SOME

ANY and SOME are used interchangeably. The preference of name and ease of use is up to the user. When used with a subquery, the condition in the subquery is true if ANY or SOME of the conditions are met.

Example:

```
SELECT * FROM customers WHERE city = ANY (SELECT
    city FROM salesreps)
```

BETWEEN OPERATOR

This command is used for locating data values within a range.

Example:

```
SELECT invid, custid, totamt FROM sales WHERE totamt
    BETWEEN 150.00 AND 250.00
```

CHANGING DATA VALUES

The following examples show ways to change the data values in a row.

Example 1:

```
UPDATE salesreps SET commiss = .15
```

Example 2:

```
UPDATE salesreps SET hiredate = 5/5/89 WHERE hiredate =
    5/4/89
```

COMPOUND CONDITIONS

Compound conditions include AND, OR, and NOT. The AND condition must include both conditions in the query, the OR may include one condition OR the other, and the NOT looks for conditions NOT equal to those in the query.

Example 1 (where both conditions must be met):

```
SELECT repid, totamt FROM sales WHERE totamt < 100.00
    AND invid >= 2/1/90
```

Example 2 (where one condition or the other must be met):

```
SELECT totamt, invid, invdate FROM sales WHERE totamt >
    300.00 OR custid = 20
```

COUNT

The following example shows the COUNT and SUM aggregate functions as discussed in Part 4 used as part of a command that groups views.

Example:

```
CREATE VIEW dailytot AS SELECT invdate, COUNT
(DISTINCT repid), SUM (DISTINCT netamt), SUM (DISTINCT tax,
(SUM DISTINCT totamt) FROM sales GROUP BY invdate
```

CREATING AN INDEX

An index may be created on any column. Its primary purpose is to make retrieval during queries a faster process.

Example:

```
CREATE INDEX ON customers custid
```

CREATING A PRIMARY KEY COLUMN

A primary key column is the one that uniquely identifies each row. This value should be one that is unique, such as social security number, customer ID, or representative ID.

Example:

```
BUILD KEY FOR custid IN customers
```

CREATING A TABLE

This command creates a base table including the table name, the columns, column type, column width, and assigns any restrictions necessary to the column.

Example:

```
CREATE TABLE customers custid INTEGER NOT NULL,
    fname TEXT(20) NOT NULL, address TEXT(25), city
    TEXT(15), state TEXT(2)
```

CREATING A VIEW

A collection of values taken from various base tables or one base table. A view table does not contain any of its own data but rather is a combination of various base table data values.

Example:

```
CREATE VIEW wacustomers AS SELECT * FROM customers
    WHERE state = 'WA'
```

DELETING ROWS

This command will delete an entire row from a table. In the example below, a condition is placed on which row will be deleted (the one with a repid of 3). Giving such conditions as all repids greater than 0 would result in deleting all rows from a table.

Example:

```
DELETE FROM salesreps WHERE repid = 3
```

DISTINCT

DISTINCT is used to avoid redundant data being pulled from tables during a query. If two or more rows contain the same information, DISTINCT will retrieve only one of those rows.

Example:

```
SELECT DISTINCT repid FROM sales
```

This command will avoid selecting redundant or duplicate data values.

DROPPING A TABLE

Using this command, you can drop a table from the database.

Example:

```
DROP TABLE salesreps
```

NOTE: You can only drop a table after all rows have been removed with the DELETE command.

EXISTS WITH CORRELATED SUBQUERIES

The EXISTS command is used to make sure that matching columns contain the same value. This example shows EXISTS in use with a subquery. Placing EXISTS prior to a subquery creates a true condition if one or more rows are found during the subquery.

Example:

```
SELECT fname, address, city FROM customers WHERE
    EXISTS (SELECT * FROM customers WHERE state =
    'AK')
```

GROUP BY AND ORDER BY CLAUSE

GROUP BY and ORDER BY allow the user to order a column as a subset of another.

Example 1:

```
SELECT repid, MAX(totamt) FROM sales GROUP BY repid
```

This example also locates the maximum value from the **totamt** column. It groups the results by **repid**.

Example 2:

```
SELECT repid, netamt, SUM(netamt*.07) FROM sales
    GROUP BY repid, netamt ORDER BY invid
```

This command will produce results showing the repid and netamt.

GROUPING VIEWS

This command allows you to group a particular column within a view.

Example:

```
CREATE VIEW dailytot AS SELECT invdate, COUNT
    (DISTINCT repid), SUM (DISTINCT netamt), SUM
    (DISTINCT tax), SUM (DISTINCT totamt) FROM sales
    GROUP BY invdate
```

HAVING CLAUSE

This command performs a search that recognizes entire groups of conditions at a time rather than one row at a time, as with the WHERE clause.

Example:

```
SELECT invdate, MAX(totamt) FROM sales GROUP BY
    invdate HAVING MAX(totamt) > 200.00
```

IN OPERATOR

This operator allows the user to locate a string of data values without writing a lengthy command.

Example:

```
SELECT * FROM customers WHERE city IN ('Kirkland',
    'Redmond', 'Eugene')
```

INSERTING VALUES IN A VIEW

You can add new values into a view through the base table. When you add new rows of data using the INSERT command, the new values will automatically be inserted into the view as well.

```
INSERT into sales VALUES
    (117,3/10/90,2,12,224.32,54.00,278.32)
```

JOINING TABLES

This command joins two or more tables in a view.

Example:

```
CREATE VIEW invday AS SELECT invdate, totamt,
    a.repfname FROM salesreps a, sales b WHERE a.repid =
    b.repid
```

LIKE OPERATOR

The LIKE operator is applied to TEXT or CHARACTER types only. This command is used when all of the parts of a data value are not known.

Example:

```
SELECT * FROM customers WHERE city LIKE ‘S%’
```

NULL VALUES IN A COLUMN

Null values are inserted into a column using the INSERT command when a data value is unknown. In the following example, the city is, at this time, unknown.

Example:

```
INSERT INTO customers VALUES (14,’Dale Glenn’,‘2518
    25th N.E.’,NULL,‘WA’)
```

QUERYING A VIEW

You can see the contents of a view just as you would any other base table.

Example:

```
SELECT * FROM wacustomers WHERE city = ‘Seattle’
```

REMOVING AN INDEX

The following command removes an index on a column of a base table.

Example:

```
DROP INDEX commiss IN salesreps
```

In this example **commiss** is the name of the index.

REPLACING NULL VALUES

Null values are inserted into columns where the data value is unknown. Usually this condition is temporary and the null value will need to be replaced. The SET command is used to replace the null value of city in the following UPDATE.

Example:

```
UPDATE customers SET city = 'Redmond' WHERE custid =
   14
```

This command assumes that the **city** column of **custid** 14 was previously identified as NULL and showed a value of -0-.

RETRIEVING ALL COLUMNS

This command allows the user to look at all columns of a base table or a view. Sometimes the number of columns is greater than can be viewed at one time on the screen, in which case it would be necessary to retrieve specific columns from the table.

Example:

```
SELECT * FROM customers
```

RETRIEVING COLUMNS IN A SPECIFIC ORDER

Columns do not always have to be viewed on the screen in the same order in which they were originally entered. You have the option of looking at columns in any order with variations of the following SELECT command.

Example:

```
SELECT state, fname, custid FROM customers
```

In this example this is not the order in which the columns were originally entered.

RETRIEVING SPECIFIC COLUMNS

This command is similar to retrieving columns in a specific order. In this instance, however, it is assumed that you would like to see the columns in their original order, only not necessarily every column of the table. This is especially useful when the table contains too many columns to fit on the width of your screen.

Example:

```
SELECT custid, name, state FROM customers
```

SUBQUERIES

Subqueries are performed so that multiple conditions may be met during a query. The inner condition is met (found to be true) first and then the outer condition is performed.

Example:

```
SELECT * FROM customers WHERE custid IN (SELECT
    custid FROM sales WHERE totamt < 200.00)
```

UPDATABLE VIEWS

Restrictions to updates are discussed in Part 4. Any updates made to a view are also made to the base table.

```
UPDATE wacustomers SET fname = 'Lloyd Olsen' WHERE
    fname = 'Lloyd Ohlsen'
```

UPDATING DATA VALUES

The UPDATE command is used to change values in a row. This can be done in one of several ways.

Example 1, a single column:

```
UPDATE salesreps SET commiss = .15
```

Example 2, specific rows:

```
UPDATE salesreps SET hiredate = 5/5/89 WHERE repid = 14
```

Example 3, multiple columns:

```
UPDATE sales SET invid = 117, invdate = 2/20/90, custid = 25
    WHERE totamt = 97.29
```

Example 4, with expressions:

```
UPDATE sales SET tax = netamt *.06 WHERE netamt >
    200.00
```

UPDATING MULTIPLE COLUMNS

This command updates more than a single column at a time.

Example 1:

```
UPDATE sales SET invid = 117, invdate = 2/20/90, custid = 25
    WHERE totamt = 97.29
```

Example 2:

```
UPDATE sales SET tax = netamt * .06 WHERE netamt >
    200.00
```

VIEWS OF ALL COLUMNS

This command is used to create a view of specific conditions within a base table.

Example:

```
CREATE VIEW wacustomers AS SELECT * FROM customers
    WHERE state = 'WA'
```

This particular command created a view called **wacustomers** from the **customers** base table for all customers living in the state of Washington (WA).

See also CREATING A VIEW

VIEWS OF SPECIFIC COLUMNS

This command is used to view selected columns from a table.

Example:

```
CREATE VIEW hired AS SELECT repid, repfname, hiredate
    FROM salesreps
```

WHERE

WHERE is actually a clause within a SQL command, but it is so often implemented that reference is made to it within this section. It is used to restrict the output during a query.

Example 1:

```
SELECT invid, netamt FROM sales WHERE netamt > 200.00
```

Example 2:

```
SELECT * FROM sales WHERE netamt > 200.00
```

APPENDIX II
GLOSSARY OF TERMS

PREVIEW

Included in this glossary are terms as they are defined in relation to SQL and R:BASE and as terms that have been used or mentioned in this text.

Alphanumeric

Consisting of both alphabetic and numeric symbols.

Application

A menu-driven set of one or more procedures or command files performing a specific series of tasks.

Arguments

Parts of a command that can change for each entry.

Ascending order

Sorting in an order from lowest to highest (such as 1 to 50, A to Z). Sorting follows the order of ASCII character codes. Ascending is the R:BASE default sorting order.

ASCII

American Standard Code for Information Interchange. A widely used computer character set in which each letter, number, and symbol has a unique numeric value. Most computers can read the ASCII character set. An ASCII file is a file that contains only characters from this character set.

ASCII delimited file

An ASCII file in which individual fields in a record are separated with a delimited character such as a comma (,) or a blank.

ASCII fixed field file

An ASCII file in which the same field in each record has the same length, regardless of the number of characters in the field. Also called a columnar text file.

Character

A single printable letter (A-Z or a-z), numeral (0-9), or symbol (such as #, $, %) used to represent data. Includes invisible characters such as space, tab, and carriage return.

Column

A specific piece of information defined for a database table. In some products called a field or attribute.

Command

An instruction to the computer, entered from the keyboard or a file. This can be a word abbreviation, or a character that directs the system to perform a predefined operation.

Command word

The full name or abbreviation of an R:BASE command, such as SELECT, SET VAR, and RBEDIT. Command words are shown in syntax diagrams in uppercase letters.

Common column

A column in two or more tables that has the same name, data type, and, if TEXT or NUMERIC, the same size.

Computed column

A column whose value R:BASE calculates, based on an expression defined for the column.

Condition

A specification that is either true or false. Conditions are used in WHERE clauses and in the IF, WHILE, and SWITCH commands.

Connecting Operators

Operators that connect conditions in a WHERE clause. The connecting operators are AND, AND NOT, OR, and OR NOT. (Called simply *operators* in this text.)

Cursor

On the screen, a movable marker or line that designates the next point of character entry or change. In a command file, a pointer to a row in a table or view.

Data

Facts, numbers, letters, and symbols stored in the computer. Data can be thought of as the basic elements of information used, created, or otherwise processed by an application program.

Database

A collection of logical groups of data, stored in one or more files, used to perform a task.

Data types

Recognized formats in which data can be represented to R:BASE: CHARACTER, CURRENCY, DATE, DECIMAL, DOUBLE, FLOAT, INTEGER, NOTE, NUMERIC, REAL, SMALLINT, TEXT, and TIME.

Delimiter

A character that marks the end of a unit of data or separates items in a list. The R:BASE default delimiter is a comma.

Descending order

Sorting in an order from highest to lowest (such as 50 to 1, Z to A). Sorting follows the reverse order of ASCII character codes.

Expression

A calculation that produces a single value as the result.

File

Data that is stored on a disk and given a unique file name. An R:BASE database is stored in three operating system files: dbname1.rbf, dbname2.rbf, and dbname3.rbf (where dbname is the name of the database).

Function

A function is a small program that performs one specific task. R:BASE has several types of functions (some of which are recognizable SQL commands used in this text). SELECT functions are used in the SELECT command and in other commands that contain a GROUP BY, HAVING or WHERE clause. COMPUTE functions are used in the COMPUTE, SET VARIABLE, and CROSSTAB commands.

Indexed column

A column for which R:BASE maintains a list of locations for the data stored in that column. Used to increase the efficiency with which R:BASE sorts and finds data.

Linking column

A column in one table that contains the same values as a column in one or more other tables. Linking columns can be two columns with the same name, data type, and size (if TEXT or NUMERIC); or two columns with different names but compatible data types.

Menu

List of options from which to choose.

Null

A representation consisting of one to four characters that identifies the absence of data or when a value does not apply. The R:BASE default is -0-.

Numeric data types

When it appears in lowercase letters, numeric refers to data types that enable you to manipulate numeric values using arithmetic operators. The following are numeric data types: CURRENCY, DECIMAL, DOUBLE, FLOAT, INTEGER, NUMERIC, REAL, SMALLINT.

Operand

A column, variable, string, or value acted on by an operator and combined with another operand to form an expression. In the expression x + y, x and y are operands and + is the operator.

Operator

A symbol (such as +, - , *, or /) representing an operation to be performed on one or more columns, values, variables, or strings. Used throughout R:BASE, especially in expressions and WHERE and HAVING clauses.

Program

A series of instructions in either binary or ASCII format that performs a specific task.

R:BASE

The Microrim database management system incorporating SQL and R:BASE commands.

Record

The equivalent of an R:BASE row in an external file.

Relational database

A database in which data is stored in a set of tables; linking columns among the tables allow for multiple-table operations.

Row

The data defined by a set of columns in a table. Some relational database products refer to a row as a record.

SQL (Structured Query Language)

A standard language for database definition, display, and manipulation. R:BASE provides the complete ANSI Level 2 SQL, which includes SQL enhancements developed by IBM for its DB2 mainframe database language.

Table

Representation of storage in a database. Composed of columns and rows.

Variable

A symbol that can assume a succession of values.

View

A collection of columns drawn from up to five existing tables or views. Use a view to retrieve current data from one to five tables or views.

WHERE clause

Used to qualify or restrict the rows affected by an operation or command.

APPENDIX III
SQL COMMAND REFERENCE

PREVIEW

This appendix shows the syntax of SQL commands. Use this reference for guidelines in constructing SQL commands discussed in this text.

BUILD KEY

BUILD KEY FOR colname IN tblname

CREATE INDEX

CREATE [UNIQUE] INDEX ON <table name> (<column list>)

CREATE INDEX ON tblname colname

CREATE TABLE

CREATE TABLE <table name> <column name> <data type>(size) <column constraint>, <column name 2> . . .

CREATE TABLE tblname 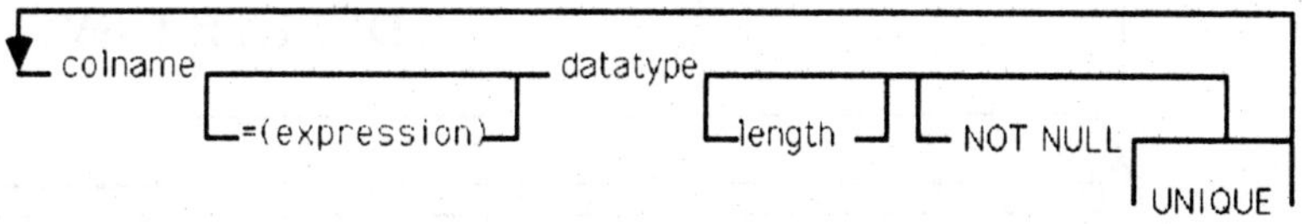 colname =(expression) datatype length NOT NULL UNIQUE

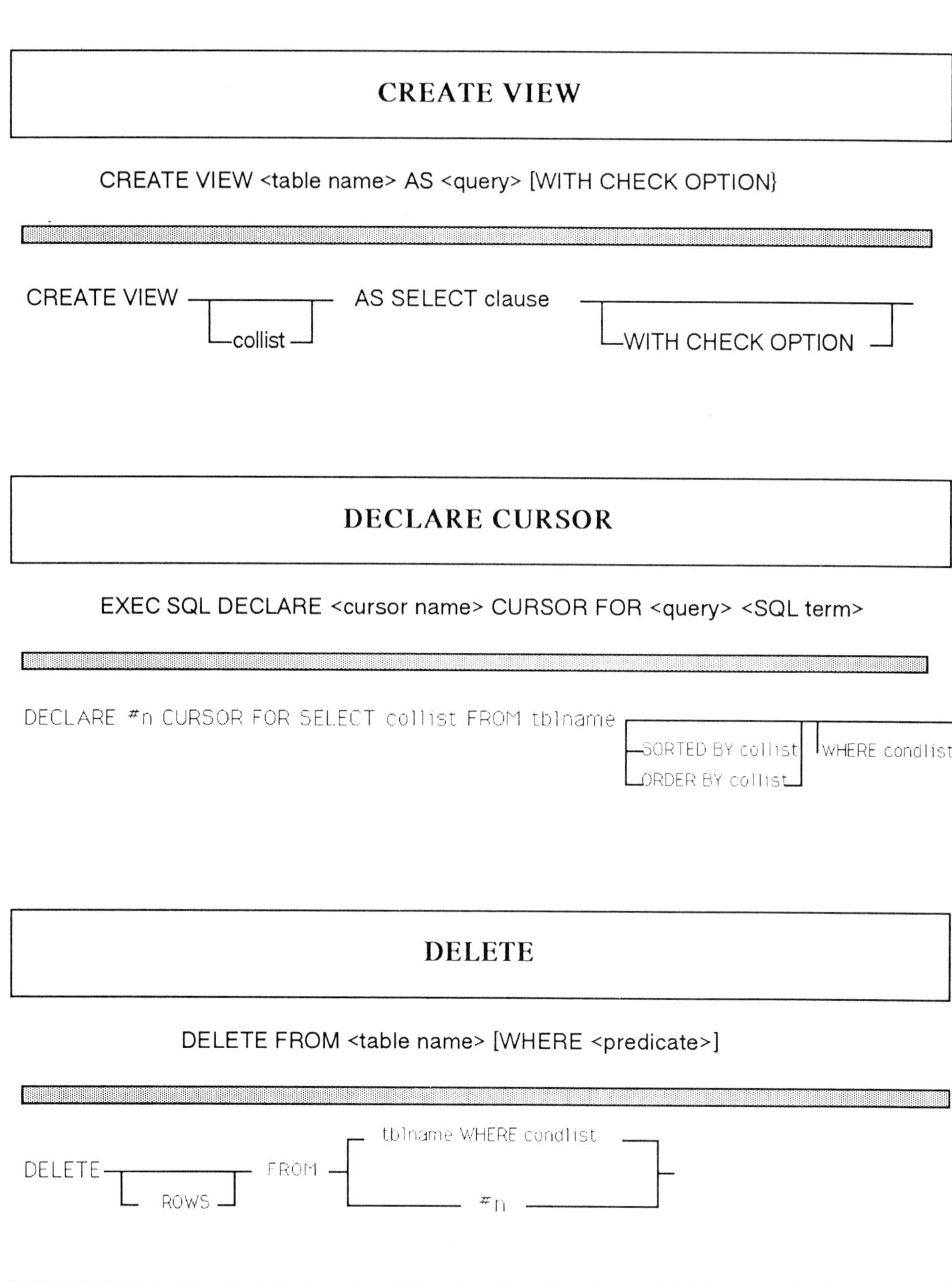

CREATE VIEW

CREATE VIEW <table name> AS <query> [WITH CHECK OPTION}

DECLARE CURSOR

EXEC SQL DECLARE <cursor name> CURSOR FOR <query> <SQL term>

DELETE

DELETE FROM <table name> [WHERE <predicate>]

DELETE KEY

DELETE KEY FOR colname IN tblname

DROP

DROP INDEX <table name>

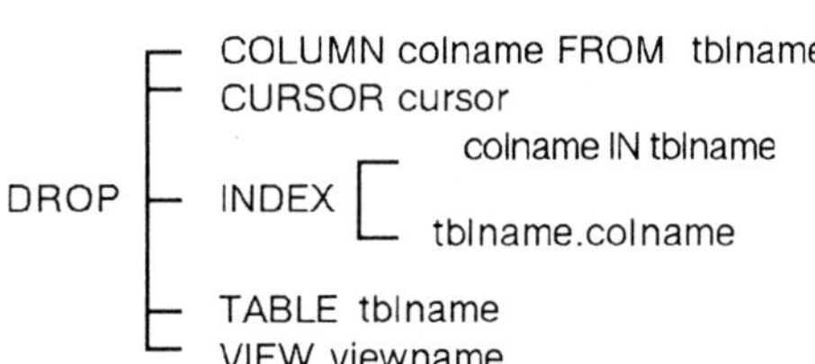

EXEC SQL

EXEC SQL <embedded SQL command> <SQL term>

FETCH

EXEC SQL FETCH <cursor name> INTO <host-variable list> <SQL term>

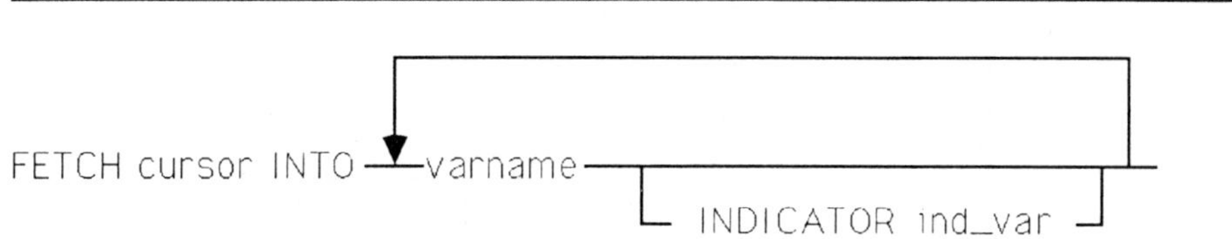

INSERT

INSERT INTO <table name> [(<column list>)] VALUES (<value list>) | <query>

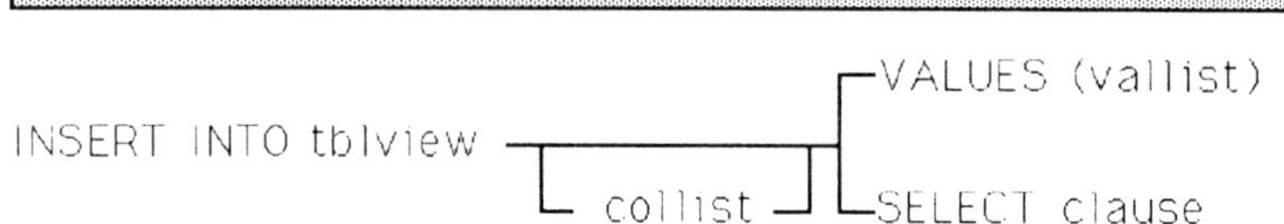

OPEN CURSOR

EXEC SQL OPEN CURSOR <cursor name> <SQL term>

SELECT and SELECT DISTINCT

SELECT {[DISTINCT | ALL] <value expression> . . . .} | * [INTO <host variable list> (*embedded only*)] FROM <table> . . l. . . [WHERE <predicate>] [GROUP BY <grouping column> . . . .] [HAVING <predicate>] [ORDER BY <ordering column> [ASC|DESC] . . . .]

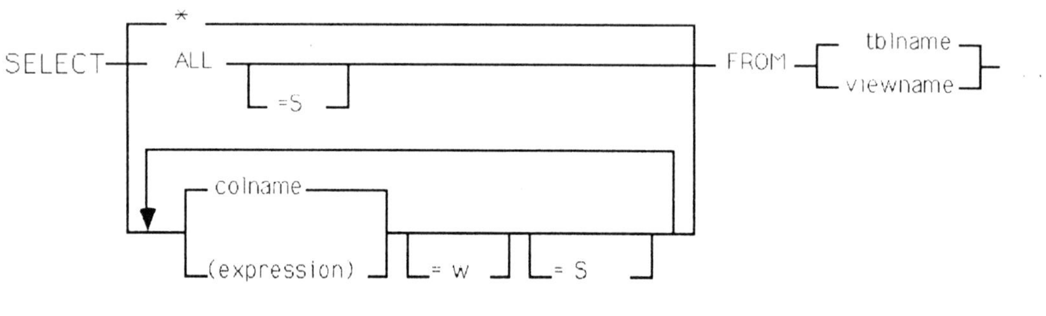

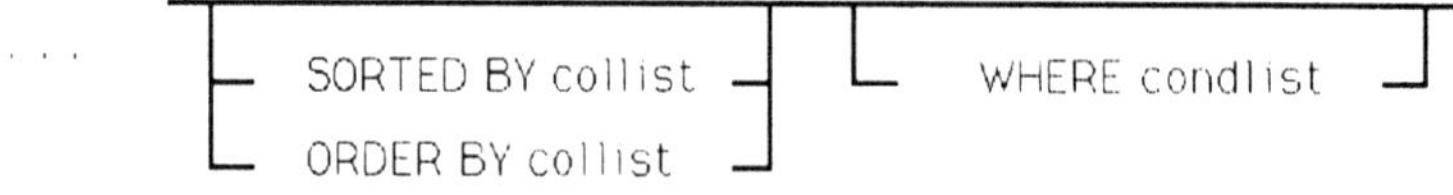

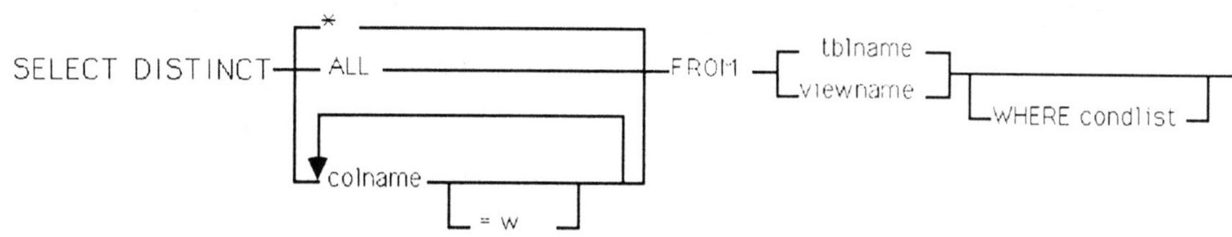

UPDATE

UPDATE <table name> SET {<column name> = <value expression> } ., . . .
{[WHERE <predicate>];}

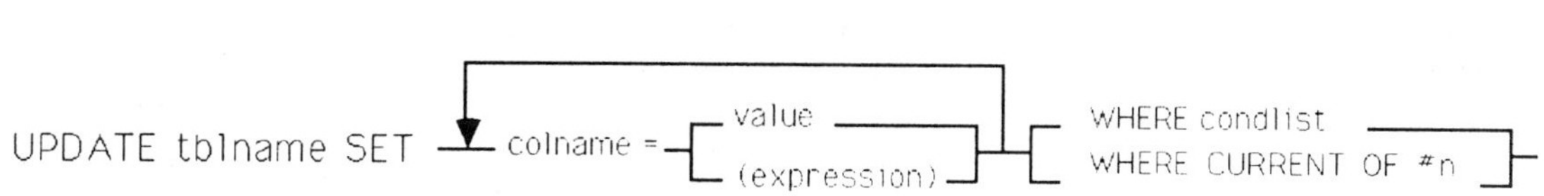

WHERE clause

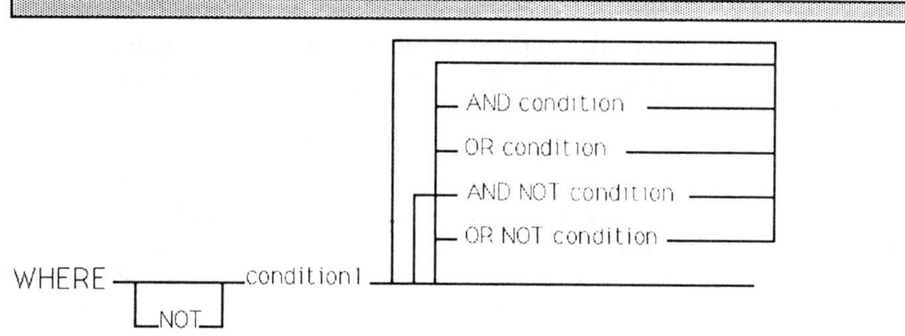

Conditions are:

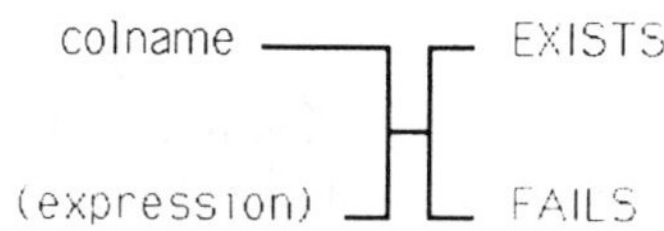

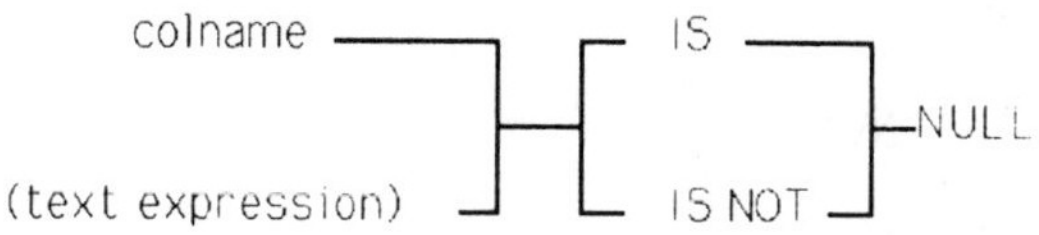

INDEX